Hi Audrey,

Thank you so much for your years of support.
I pray that this book will enlighten, inspire and cause elevation in your career.

Be Blessed

Camille B. Hall

GUIDANCE FOR YOUR JOURNEY

AN ENTREPRENEUR'S MANUAL
FOR SUCCESS IN BUSINESS

CAMILLA RENAY
TERRELL

CAMILLA RENAY TERRELL
To book Camilla Renay Terrell for a speaking engagement
or to host a business-training event in your area, please
contact the author at:
camillawithenvision@gmail.com
(404) 245-4055

SUCCESS & BEYOND GLOBAL ENTERPRISES,
PUBLISHER
info@success-beyond.com
PO BOX 1753
DOUGLASVILLE GEORGIA,
(919) 673-1707

ISBN:151963241x

Edited by Able & Willing Editing
www.awe-edit.com
info@awe-edit.com

Printed in the United States of America

PREFACE

In this journey called life, most of us aspire to be successful. Success, generally speaking, means to "live the American Dream", to climb the corporate ladder, to soar in the market as an entrepreneur, or to make a lot of money doing what one loves to do. As a successful entrepreneur, business coach/mentor, and international leadership trainer, I hear the professional hopes and dreams of thousands of people each year. The top two desires of most of the people I have employed, trained, or mentored over the past twenty-eight years, has been to work a job that makes them happy and to make a lot of money. That's not too much to ask. Right? I would think not.

Unless you were born into a wealthy family, married a wealthy partner, received a substantial inheritance, a settlement, or won the lottery; I assume you work to make a living for you and your family. I imagine that on a daily basis, you exchange your time and skills for money to pay bills and purchase the things you need or want. This is normal—you work to live. Right? Well, I say it is not normal. I propose, instead of working to live, that we live to work, that is if we are working, doing the things we are created, designed and destined to do. I believe in our life span here on earth, we should make the most of our time by finding the things that make us happy personally and professionally; then do them with no regrets.

Money is a valuable resource but so is time. Time however, is an irreplaceable resource, that when lost can never be regained. Money on the other hand, can be lost and recovered quickly and easily by various means. The reality is the average person spends most of their time working, doing something they do not enjoy. The time we spend working is time spent away from the people and things that bring us joy such as a spouse, children, or loved ones, all with the goal of making money. Most people work at least eight hours a day while others work up to sixteen hours a day. We put this type of dedication into our jobs and careers because most often it is necessary, we need money. But if making money is the only reason you work, then at some point, you will become frustrated, worn out, unhappy, unfulfilled, feel void and depressed.

Everyone works either a job they hate or love. Since most of your time is dedicated to working, why not make a concerted effort to devote your time, your most valuable resource, to doing what brings you joy and wealth? Why not pursue a dream job or start the business that has been on your mind for years? Just think of the happiness that would come from building your life around doing the things that motivate you; having the freedom to be your own boss, or the fulfillment that would come from serving your purpose here on earth. AND, being successful or making a great living while achieving your dream.

If we were honest, we would admit there is a bit of trepidation in the idea of pursuing our passions. There is a considerable amount of hesitation in stepping outside the box to do what is in our hearts rather than just doing what "pays the bills". There is doubt regarding the outcome of taking the road less traveled, marching to the beat of our own drum instead of accepting the marching orders given by society, teachers, or well-intended parents. There is fear associated with following our dreams, as often our dreams don't lead down what others may deem a logical path.

Many times, our dreams seem "illogical" to most and often lead us into unchartered territory causing us to have to believe in ourselves like never before, use our faith like never before, pull out untapped skills and talents and try things many others in our lives may never have tried before.

The fact is, you are just one decision away from a complete life change from being 'here' at this moment and being 'there' the next. One decision can change the entire course of your life. It can take you from living paycheck-to-paycheck just getting by, to living an abundant life and acquiring financial wealth to share with others. One decision determines if you achieve your goals, follow your dreams and pursue your life passions. The decision is simply that I WILL DO IT. I will achieve my goals, live my dreams, and pursue my passions.

We are all going somewhere in life and our decisions are the driving force which transport us. The decisions we make today, drive us to our tomorrow.

That is why this book is so important. We all need guidance or advice from those with wisdom and experience to help us make sound decisions. There are times we need confirmation, or signs that we are on the right path or are going in the right direction, because there are so many roads that would appear to lead to success, but instead lead to nowhere. Just like when traveling in a vehicle, we need specific directions to guide us to our intended destination. We need the GPS to lead us with turn-by-turn directions to ensure we make it to our desired location in the most expedient time possible.

I wrote this book to push you, to assist you in making a decision to live your dreams and to give you professional GUIDANCE FOR YOUR JOURNEY, leading you directly to the destination of success in business.

If you ask any world leader, business pioneer, or enlightened person noted for living their dreams or achieving greatness, they will tell you there are foundational principles to achieving success. One principle is to get knowledge and understanding about anything you wish to do; seek out wisdom from those who have been where you are preparing to go, get insight and guidance from experts and then apply the information learned immediately. By obtaining proven, tried by fire advice in any given subject, you save yourself the trouble of wasting a lot of time by avoiding preventable mistakes.

Instead of living by trial and error, why not accelerate your journey by simply learning life-long lessons in a matter of minutes just by reading a book?

Get to your destination more quickly by getting GPS assistance—GUIDANCE FOR YOUR JOURNEY and enjoy the ride!

TABLE OF CONTENTS

INTRODUCTION

Guidance is defined as advice or information aimed at resolving a problem or difficulty, especially as given by someone in authority. Synonyms for guidance include advice, counsel, direction, instruction, enlightenment and information. Guidance also refers to directing or redirecting of the motion or position of something or someone. Journey is defined as the act of traveling from one place to another or moving or going somewhere. A distance to be traveled that takes a specific amount of time.

So, combining both definitions, the aim of *GUIDANCE FOR YOUR JOURNEY* is to enlighten you. To give you divine direction relating to finding the shortest path to pursuing your professional purpose and becoming successful in your field of choice. This book will assist you in identifying the signs along the way that confirm either that you are on the right path or that you are heading down the wrong road and need to detour, backtrack, or start all over.

This book will ignite you to "pursue your passions and not just a paycheck". To resolve inner conflicts, doubts, or fears that would prevent you from taking the next step in your career or in launching your new business. Every journey begins with one single step. So, "Let the journey begin"!

GUIDANCE FOR YOUR JOURNEY is the perfect business resource for Hair Salon Owners, Stylists, Make-Up Artists, Estheticians, Fashion Designers, Massage Therapists, and Entrepreneurs who desire to launch a new business or take an established enterprise to the next level. This book will help sharpen personal and professional skills, increase marketability and productivity as well as teach you how to make a lot of money doing what you love.

This book is also ideal for college students, stay-at-home parents, or those wishing to "try something new", as it identifies an array of viable business opportunities within the Beauty Industry. It also helps stimulate entrepreneurial-minded individuals to take advantage of potentially untapped areas of wealth. To achieve any desired goal in life, such as obtaining a new job in a Day Spa, becoming a celebrity stylist, or owning your own product line, we must be honest about where we currently are in relation to where we desire to be in the future. Then, we must identify the tools and resources we currently possess to achieve the desired goal as well as those we do not.

Following a plan of action is necessary and we must strategically map out the steps required to realize our goals. A good starting point to achieving a business goal is to utilize a vision board. On that board, create a road map or plan of action to get to the next destination. The next step is to conduct a personal and professional assessment, or inventory prior to beginning the plan. Why start with an inventory? It is necessary to know what you already possess to complete a task or goal in relation to what you currently lack. Knowing this information allows you to identify your strengths and weaknesses, set a realistic timeframe and more accurately map out a plan to acquire or develop the skills, tools or resources you lack to achieve your goal.

I believe we are all divinely creative beings that come to earth equipped with skills, talents, and natural gifts for a purpose. The personal "equipment for success" is inside each of us. When we learn the abilities we possess, they give us guidance on what we should do for a living. They also give us insight on locating business opportunities and wisdom for creating new streams of wealth for our families.

Identifying your natural gifts, talents, and skills, then mapping a career path based upon them will automatically position you to excel in the workforce or in business in general. I also believe obtaining targeted education that develops your gifts, talents, and skills as it relates to being successful in any craft will expedite the process of bringing your business vision to fruition. I've seen it happen in my own life and in the lives of countless others. Pursuing your passions instead of pursuing paychecks is a principle that really works!

At its core, this book is about living a life of passion and staying in love with your craft through the art of professional development and training. When you love what you do, you create an atmosphere of joy, peace, and positivity. In this type of positively charged atmosphere, new ideas are free to flow, which increases your creativity. When you increase your creativity, your productivity generally increases. An environment of creativity and productivity will always yield increased product demand, clientele, and revenue. This is a core principle for achieving success in any area of business.

My goal is to teach you fundamental principles of success in business while giving you over 25 years of tried by fire "know-how" to develop a business idea, launch a new venture, or expand an existing enterprise. My aim is to help you use your time wisely, because once time is used, it can never be regained. It's gone forever! You do not want to waste time simply going through the motions in life, just getting by, or working a job you hate. That is merely existing. I want to show you how to do what you love and make a lot of money at the same time.

Remember, chase after your passion not paychecks, then the paychecks will chase you!

THE JOURNEY CALLED LIFE

Life is a journey and ultimately our goal is to arrive at a place of happiness, peace, abundance and fulfillment. Before beginning any journey, it is necessary to have a destination in mind. Without a clear destination, we will end up going in circles and wasting time.

After defining a clear destination for your journey, you must prepare the proper provisions for the trip. Often times we pack unnecessary things that take up needed space, weighing us down, and ultimately slowing us down in our travels. Can you recall a time you brought too many bags and wished you had left those huge three extra suitcases home while attempting to run through the airport dragging them in an effort to make your flight in time? Whew! They were heavy; they caused you to decrease your speed, and tired you out as you tried to lug them around.

The same concept applies to our life and travels. We have a destination in mind, an ideal time set to get there, but we often carry around old baggage that slows us down. The old baggage could be self-defeating thought patterns, old ways of thinking about the business, the world, negative words people have spoken about us which made us feel inadequate, or fear because of our past mistakes or failures that made us doubt the probability of future success. When we carry this mental baggage around, it takes up space and lessens our ability to "pack" helpful information. Honestly if something is not helpful to you, it's harmful. As a man thinks in his heart, so is he (Proverbs 23:7). This means that we become the sum total of our inner most thoughts. As such, we must evaluate how we think about ourselves, the direction of our lives, and plan for our futures. What have you packed for your journey?

To be a good traveler, you must PLAN AHEAD. Nothing just happens and you will not become a huge success in business by osmosis. You need to research your intended destination then create a plan to get there in the shortest amount of time possible. This requires vision and faith. Then, it requires setting a date, packing the necessary items, removing distractions that would pull you off course, and following the road signs along the way.

Our intended destination in business is success. I define success in business as doing what you love, making enough money to meet all your needs, having enough to invest and give freely to those in need. You are able to live comfortably and save enough so you may set your children up for successful futures. Being successful is living each day feeling happy and fulfilled because you KNOW that you are operating in your purpose and living out your passions. Following your dreams, whatever they are, and seeing them through to fruition, makes you a success.

FIND YOUR PURPOSE

Wisdom is the principle thing, therefore, get wisdom and in all of your getting, get understanding.
Proverbs 4:7

The world contains much ancient wisdom that provides each person with answers to all of life's problems, solutions to the challenges and advice for all situations. One source of ancient wisdom is the Bible; God's road map for us to live successful lives on earth. In addition to giving us day-by-day advice, the Bible also provides fundamental principles for achieving success in everything we do. Most of the "thought" leaders around the world, no matter their religious background, would agree that there are spiritually based universal principles for success. We may not quote the text of origin the exact same way, but the principle is the same.

An example of one universal spiritual principle for success is the concept of becoming successful through self-knowledge. In essence, by connecting with your spiritual core, learning who you are, why you were created and what your divine qualities or internal capabilities are, you will ultimately become successful through divine assistance, how you think and see yourself.

Another universal principle within this same vein is that our thoughts create things and we are always in the process of creating something. By evaluating and training our thought processes, we steer our lives in the right direction and achieve our goals by focusing on our strengths as opposed to perceived weaknesses. Focusing on working on our strategy to get where we are going rather than counting the reasons why we cannot get there and thinking success rather than the possibility of failure are examples of divine wisdom.

The Scripture quoted in a previous section of the book was Proverbs 23:7, as a man thinks in his heart/mind/soul, so will he become. So, to start your journey, I would suggest you begin to think about who you would like to become since that is the way you will become that person. Thoughts create.

Thought leaders from diverse backgrounds across the globe generally agree on the basic concept of the purpose of humanity. The belief is that each and every person was created uniquely by a Divine Being or God, for a divine purpose; that we are all given assignments to complete while here on earth that will ultimately help another person along their journey to fulfill their purpose. Additionally, I believe each person has been equipped with a special set of skills, talents, and internal gifts that aid them in successfully fulfilling their purpose in life. Often times, we fulfill our purposes through our business efforts, that is why it is so important to make sure we understand what motivates, inspires and brings us joy as those are clues to what our assignments are, both personally and professionally.

BY FINDING YOUR PASSIONS, YOU WILL FIND YOUR PURPOSE

God created everything and everyone with and for a purpose. You were birthed into this earthly existence to complete certain things while you are here. A few examples may be to open a homeless shelter, to develop a cure for cancer, or invent a product that would help the world in some way.

If you research people like Albert Einstein, Oprah Winfrey, or President Barak Obama, you will find all these legendary innovators state they had a longing to do something great for humanity. Like solve a massive problem, pave the way for their families or give of themselves to the world creatively by using their skills, talents, and inner gifts.

If you begin to think about causes you support, community issues you would like to resolve, or even things you like to do to help others, you will begin to discover your passions, the things that make you happy and bring fulfillment.

We all want to be happy and feel fulfilled, but sometimes we are misguided about where true happiness and fulfillment come from. It is never just about you. The fulfillment in locating and pursuing your passions comes through serving a greater good, not just living day to day, worrying about how to pay a bill or if you will have what you need to survive. By thinking of career and business development as a means to serve a greater good, you place yourself in forward motion, moving towards achieving success in that area because of the selfless intent. This my friend, is another huge wisdom nugget and spiritual principle, when you give, you get. So as you decide on a career or business venture, make sure your motives are pure and not self-centered.

There is nothing wrong with desiring to be wealthy, but if your intention is to hoard money, buy expensive clothes and accumulate material things; not serving a greater purpose other than yourself, then you may want to rethink the goal. When your inner most desire is to be successful so you may help others along the way, the universe always supports that request and your business plans will, without a doubt, prosper.

THE JOURNEY BEGINS

This book is entitled, *GUIDANCE FOR YOUR JOURNEY,* because I believe life is a journey and there is a day-by-day process for us all to become the person we were created to be, personally and professionally. There is a procedure and process for anything you desire to do in life, and once you understand the process, it makes the journey easier. My goal is to provide practical advice, spiritual principles, and more than three decades of personal experience in successful business operations to prevent you from making careless mistakes or wasting time as you take the next step in realizing your dreams.

The wisdom and universal principles provided in this book applies to all professions, business concepts, and entrepreneurial ventures. For example, the person who decided to become a make-up artist, a boutique owner, or a stylist, didn't do so by chance. They chose those specific areas of service because they possess certain talents and gifts in those areas.

Has anyone ever told you something like, "You are such a natural at designing clothes?" "You can do hair with your eyes closed." "You are a gifted massage therapist?" Well those are just a few examples of how others sometimes identify with your gifting more directly than you do at times. The compliments that you can do something "with your eyes closed" or that "you are a natural" at something speaks to what they perceive as your innate ability. Innate abilities are things we do not have to "try hard" to do, or things we do effortlessly but flawlessly. Those innate abilities my friend, I propose, is your area of gifting.

Combining Gifts, Talents, and Business Ideas

In basic terms, if you have a vision for business, you are equipped with natural gifts that will aid you along the way to seeing the vision come to pass. Proverbs 18:16 says that your gifts will make room for you, place you before great men and women of notoriety and power to cause you to be more successful.

It is interesting to note that the Bible does not say that a man's education makes room for him, but that his gift does. What you are actually known for is your gift; God has put gifts or talents in every person, and the world will "create a space" or a "market" for that gift. This is a key principle for achieving success in business. Once you fully understand this principle, you won't work as hard, but you will work smarter to tap into the areas within yourself that will lead you to divine connections, more business clients, new market opportunities, which all equal the potential for additional streams of income.

Although this book will train you on the academic necessities, business acumen, and professional skill sets required in achieving your goals, I will continue to emphasize the importance of identifying and utilizing your natural talents or gifts as a main plan of action.

There must be a thirst for greatness—a thirst for success; when one begins to move towards their purposed journey, the thirst begins to be quenched.

Camilla Renay Terrell

We are all traveling to get from one place to the next. The way we get to where we are going in the shortest amount of time, is to pay attention to the road signs, follow directions and listen to wisdom and instruction. The road signs, advice, wisdom and instructions come to us in various ways. They come through reviewing the pattern of your life experiences, the quiet voice that speaks to you, the direct advice from respected individuals with professional and life experience, and messages that seem to speak directly to us through songs, movies, and books. If you read carefully, I believe you will complete this book and receive direct Guidance for Your Journey and be able to apply fundamental principles for achieving success in business.

WISDOM FROM MY JOURNEY

There are always people and experiences in your life that teach you powerful lessons. I did not grow up wealthy. As a matter of fact, I was poor. I might even venture to say I was PO! This means, that I had much less than the average "poor" person. For this reason, I believe there was a burning desire or thirst inside of me to make it big and become successful, because I never ever, ever, wanted to be poor again. I wanted to have enough money to take care of my children and myself and not worry about where our next meal would come from. Moreover, I wanted to live lavishly, to have all of the nice material things I missed as a child.

I recall a pivotal moment in my past when I discovered I was an entrepreneur and had no desire to work for another person. That realization is where my journey began. My Aunt Sadie Mae Dobbins, who is very special to me, gave me so many nuggets of wisdom. Those nuggets influenced me greatly and changed my entire way of seeing the world around me and myself. She basically molded my mind, a poor young girl who grew up in a lil' old town in the country. She taught me to have high self-esteem, know that I was special, to always believe in my abilities despite what others say, to reach for the stars and grab hold to all my dreams.

One of the essential nuggets she gave me which changed my life was teaching me to think like a business owner instead of an employee, even if I was an employee at the time.

She also taught me to respect other people's things by treating them as if they were my own. For example, if someone let me borrow a shirt, I should take care of the shirt as if it were mine; not abuse it and to return it in the same condition I received it or better.

I bet you are wondering how these lessons my Aunt Sadie Mae taught me relate to being successful in business. Well, little did I know at the time, what seemed to be small "old-timey" suggestions by my aunt would prove to be life-altering business advice that directly aided in my success as an entrepreneur.

Case in point, I remember going in to interview for my very first job, not knowing what I wanted to do with my life for the long haul but knowing I needed to make some money to provide for myself. I entered McDonald's as a confident and capable employee. I was able to look at the opportunity from a larger scale, taking the initiative to make the work environment better and enhance the company while I was on the clock. This stemmed from hearing my aunt tell me how special I was, and how my talents would change the world. She told me I had what it took to own my own company. So, even though I did not know exactly how or when I would do all of the great things my aunt told me I was capable of, I believed her and saw endless possibilities for my life and future career.

My first day at McDonald's afforded me a new experience, an opportunity to test the waters and discover if working there was a good fit for me. Could this be my dream job? A place where I could grow and develop my skills? Would I enjoy doing my daily tasks for the rest of my life? Did I feel excited about going into work every day? Did I feel alive, motivated, and inspired while at work? The answer to all of those questions was no. I felt completely unhappy while there, like I should be doing something else.

Although I performed well and excelled at my job, I was consistently observing my environment looking for ways to make it better for the customers and staff. I was generally the leader that most people looked to for advice or help in completing their jobs. I prided myself on doing a good job, but I immediately knew that working at McDonald's for a lifetime was not for me. Just because I cooked french fries well, did not mean I should cook fries for a career. For those who find enjoyment and are fulfilled cooking fries, this statement does not apply. For me, I did the job, but was not connected to it in any way. I was thinking about doing other things while at work. This was a key indicator I was not working in my purpose.

Thankfully, because of the words of empowerment spoken into my life at a young age, I was able to envision more for my life. I saw opportunities outside of just cooking french fries even though it provided stable income for me as a young person with no other experience. Unlike some of the other young people who worked alongside me at "Mickey D's", as an employee, I saw this large corporation as a business I could actually own and operate. As such, I treated McDonald's as if I actually owned it while being employed there. I don't mean I tried to take the place over or anything, but I took the initiative to make the work environment better for everyone, to enhance the company's production while on the clock. This not only made a huge impression on the supervisors but also on all those who encountered me. Putting my best foot forward even though I knew I was not destined to work there the rest of my life, showed others my character. I kept hearing people tell me how good I would be in leadership roles. They often said I had a bright future or that I would excel in any workplace I chose. They identified skill sets in me I wasn't aware of at the time. This stop on my journey taught me so much about myself professionally.

I believe the "business owner mentality" I displayed while an employee at McDonald's, was a major contributing factor to me realizing my dream of actually becoming a business owner. By thinking and believing I could potentially own and operate a large corporation, I seemed to strive for more at every phase in my life. By always striving for more, I ended up achieving more at each phase of my life. This, my friend, is an essential quality of a successful businessperson. Think big! Always strive to excel beyond your previous achievement or current situation, have the vision and faith to see past where you are to where you want to be.

Thoughts Become Things & Your Mentality Matters

Thoughts become things and your mentality plays a major role in what happens in your life. This is why no matter where you are in relation to achieving a business goal, it's most important to see yourself arriving at your desired ending destination. See past the now. Having a clear vision and taking ownership of whatever your vision is for yourself from day one, is a necessary part of seeing your vision realized.

It is important to see the bigger picture, to expand your mind beyond your present circumstance or experience. It doesn't really matter where you start as long as you START somewhere. I propose the best place to start is with your thoughts. What you think about yourself and what you want. If you have not taken a moment to evaluate your life and current condition as it relates to "living your dreams" then that is where you start. Are you happy working your current job? Are you excited about life in general? Do you feel like you are doing what you were meant to do? What would you like to see yourself doing in 5 – 10 years?

We must consistently evaluate our lives to see if we are making progress and going in the right direction. What is the right direction? Your gut will tell you—your inner spirit. Your visions and dreams give you direction as to which path is the right one for you. Pay attention to your inner desires. Write them down and then actively plan to "just do it" someway, somehow.

My first self-evaluation took place during my work experience at McDonald's. The lessons learned there pushed me to pursue my passions and become a business owner, product innovator and entrepreneur.

Working at McDonald's made clear to me the things I did not want to do, which is the first step in understanding the things I actually did want to do. You too must figure out what you like and don't like to do with your skills and time. You must have a good idea of what you really desire to do for the rest of your life and then begin to plan for it just as you see it in your heart.

In that place of evaluation, I knew in my gut McDonald's was not my final stop, I mentally created a vision for my life. I began to lay out the things I wanted to do and entered into a personal agreement with myself to work diligently towards seeing my visions realized. I made a decision to live my dreams.

For many of us, it will take several stops on our journey before arriving at our professional destinations, while for others it will not take many stops at all. Either way, there is something to learn at every stop that will assist us in becoming better people in general growth and development. Seeing each job opportunity as a learning experience as we move forward towards what's ahead, will get you where you are going much more quickly than you may realize. If you seek to grow and excel, you will. It's all about vision, desire, and intent. The stronger your desire and intent and the clearer your vision, the faster you will move.

EMBRACE THE POSSIBILITIES

By always viewing my job assignments from the perspective of the business owner, I was able to embrace the possibility of that becoming a reality for me. Additionally, by demonstrating a high level of respect for each business establishment as if it were my own, as my Aunt Sadie Mae taught me, I always operated in terms of how I could make a lasting impact on others while working. Instead of just "working", I used my skills to serve people. My heart was to make each organization function more productively. I sought to solve problems in the work environment. These perspectives and modalities of operating professionally directly lead us to identifying our core skills, finding our passions and then effortlessly moving to pursue them.

I will ask questions throughout this book and encourage you to take the time to answer them honestly. By answering these questions, you will begin to understand what things are most important to you and the types of jobs, business ventures, or career paths would make you happy.

Finding our place of professional happiness and discovering our passion is the beginning of all business success.

Although we will delve more deeply into developing a vision for your life and business, tapping into natural gifts/talents, and finding success by becoming servant centered as opposed to work-minded, in later chapters, let us begin thinking about those topics a bit now. Ask yourself:

- What business ideas do I have that would solve a problem in the world?
- What skills do I have that would contribute to my workplace functioning more efficiently?
- What if money wasn't an issue, what jobs would I do full-time for free?

Write your answers in complete sentences in a journal or on a note pad, you will keep.

One way to answer the question, "What business ideas do I have that would solve a problem in the world?" is, *"I would like to open a Youth Center for teenage mothers that would provide job training, parenting classes, and housing assistance. The problem it would aim to address is homelessness among teenage females, high unemployment rates, and the number of babies who get a tough start because of unstable home situations with young parents".*

An answer to the question about skills that would contribute to your work environment being more efficient, could be, *"I'm organized, type fast, great with computers, and can do graphic designs"*.

For the last question, "If money wasn't an issue, what job would I do full-time for free?" Could be answered with, *"If money wasn't an issue, I would love to open a cooking school and a string of Italian restaurants all over the United States."*

These types of questions all indicate areas of passions, dreams, and natural gifts and professional skills. Knowing your heart's desires and identifying your talents will directly help you find the career path that is right for you or begin your plan to pursue an undiscovered passion in business.

Keep your journal or note pad close and continue to write down ideas and thoughts that come to mind as you read this book, no matter how random or trivial they may seem. Trust me, these notes will all prove to be signs as you travel on the road to self-discovery that will give you Guidance for Your Journey.

DON'T DESPISE HUMBLE BEGINNINGS

I worked a few odd jobs after McDonald's and they all taught me something important that aided me in becoming successful in business.

My next pit stop was Maury Regional Hospital in Tennessee. I worked as a dietician in the Café. My wisdom guide there was Ms. Diane, a supervisor who taught me a key aspect of effective networking, although that is not what she called it. She called it "putting names with faces and remembering the people who came into the cafeteria regularly". Serving food to the hospital staff was my main function. Ms. Diane impressed upon me the importance of learning all of the doctor's faces as they went through the cafeteria lines to pick up their food. They usually put their food orders on a tab and paid their bills at the end of the month.

Some staff members came up with systems that worked for them while others never had to use a system at all, they could easily recall information and names. I followed her advice and started memorizing their names as they came in using a face/picture association. I was not one of those persons with a photographic memory so I found a way to remember the names and menu choices that worked for me. I would associate specific characteristics and foods with faces. For example, Dr. Brad Pace always ordered hamburgers with no tomatoes. Since he had distinct reddish cheeks, it was easy for me to associate red cheeks with red tomatoes. So the food order was covered but I just could not remember the names well (still can't) without much effort. To solve this memory issue, I sang face-food phrases like, "Brad Pace, red face, no tomatoes".

Unbeknownst to me at the time, Ms. Diane had taught me a major aspect of becoming successful in business. How so, you ask. Well, your network is your net WORTH and the first step in establishing a business relationship is making a strong initial connection with a person. It always makes a great impression if you remember a person's name or their favorite food. So, I would say meeting new people and building new professional relationships is the number one key to operating a successful business. The more people you meet and build a relationship with, the more access you will have for business opportunities. Additionally, you are just four people away from anyone in the entire world. You never know how developing a new relationship will change your life for the better. The world is based on connectivity and people make the world go round. We all need and rely on one another to fulfill needs. I have something to offer the world and so do you. The more people you meet and the more you learn about what they have to offer or what they need; the more likely you will be able to fulfill their need or they may be able to fulfill a need you have or one for someone you know.

Some of biggest business deals are not necessarily done in the boardroom, but often are sealed during basic one-on-one conversations between two individuals who have established a relationship and have come to trust each other at some level. This is why successful people engage in so many networking events, social and professional. The idea is that by expanding your network, your personal and professional circle, you immediately increase your opportunities to gain new business. By remembering something personal about a person such as their likes or dislikes, you very quickly establish a rapport with them and open the door to building a relationship.

I still use the face/picture association memorization skill in my networking venues and have made countless key connections. These connections have led to years of extended business clients. The take away is this; everyone you meet is a potential client or business partner. If not for you directly, they may be a connection to a new client or business opportunity. From that perspective, you should always strive to be kind and show yourself friendly. Practice the art of "putting a name to a face" or at least remembering a personal detail that someone you have met has shared with you. When you meet them again or happen to reach out to them regarding business, details matter. The mere fact that you remember that "Dr. Brad Pace" doesn't like tomatoes, could ultimately make you stand out from the crowd and gain not only a business opportunity but also a lifetime friendship, which is most valuable above all.

NO MAN IS AN ISLAND

To truly be successful in life, you must see that life is about more than just yourself and actually considering the needs of others before your own propels you into your destiny personally and professionally. Although we are all traveling and finding our way, it is important to think of others and offer whatever we may have at any given to time to assist them in arriving to their destination. The concept is, when you give, you receive and what you do for others ultimately happens for you. It happens because of your intent to help, the condition of your heart being unselfish.

Even though we all face challenges in achieving goals, we should, from that place of understanding, connect with others who may be in need, to assist them in achieving their goals. It could be as little as an encouraging word to someone who is discouraged, offering information about a topic you are familiar with to a person seeking guidance, or actually taking on a mentee who could benefit from your support in one way or another.

By thinking about others, Team Universe, you put into action the principle of giving and receiving and you will experience a reciprocal effect. Your need to gain knowledge, help, or direct access to what you are seeking returns to you. I can honestly say that much of my success in business, the open doors, new opportunities, and divine assistance, came to me this way.

I initially learned this invaluable life lesson from Eddie Hickman, my basketball coach at Mt. Pleasant High School in Tennessee. He would often tell us as kids, "It's not about you, it's about the team". He'd go on to say, "No one person is an island, you are only as strong as your weakest link."

Not only did his advice assist me in activating divine universal principles that worked on my behalf for new opportunities, but he also taught me how to eventually build a strong team for my future organizations. Although I have the title of Owner/CEO, my focus is not on just me and my skills, talents and contributions to the business. My focus, remains on the team, the organization as a whole.

This wisdom nugget, being team-focused, will help you if you plan to launch a new business. It will help you stay grounded with an initial understanding that while you may have the vision, it will require others to assist you to carry and bring it to life. We all need each other in some way in life and business. Despite what it appears another person may have to offer, you should set your intentions on using what you have, whether it is knowledge, money, or direct access to an opportunity to help someone else.

I recall another voice of wisdom that watered the seed of "giving to receive" and always focusing on strengthening others as a means to advance in life and business. Ms. Georgia Palmer and her daughter Gwen Fulgam, were the owners of "Me & Mom's Beauty Salon" in Columbia, Tennessee. They taught me specifically how to recruit, select, and train new staff. When she would give me something, I would always ask her how I could repay her and she would just tell me to pay it forward. By paying it forward, she meant, helping someone else by sharing resources and information.

For example, although I was a licensed cosmetologist, I sat under Ms. Georgia Palmer and her daughter Gwen, just to gain and share knowledge. My goal was to lay aside all that I knew to learn the ins and outs of operating a successful business.

To set in motion the principle of reciprocity and propel me forward, I would teach the young ladies in their hair salon, everything I knew. I shared what I had learned from a place of giving with the understanding that in so doing, a supernatural law was initiated on my behalf. That ultimately, whatever you give, will come back into your life to meet your own needs and that when you give, you will receive. It's a divine principle that most successful people know and understand.

Now, years later, I operate by the same principle in my businesses. I teach all staff not only about the basics of cosmetology and salon ownership, but also advanced business concepts such as import and export. I seek to develop them from day one not only as hairstylists, but also as business owners and entrepreneurs. By doing so, I've seen huge success in the growth of my businesses. Growth always starts with people, with relationships, how they are formed and managed in organizations.

In growing the staff for my hair salons, I aim to respect all staff no matter their background, skill level, or length of connection to my businesses. To advance the cause of the team, growth, production and profit, I keep in mind that each person is important to the organization. Each person's individual contribution is necessary to make the business function. From this perspective, I continue to share all of my talents, skills, and life experiences with my staff to sharpen, develop, and grow them in the shortest time possible through knowledge and exposure. It is my policy that each seasoned hairstylists mentor the new hairstylists so that all persons in our organization are brought up to as high a skill level as possible. I want each person to become sharper personally and professionally. That way, the business can progress more quickly because we are all strong in the knowledge of our craft. After all, the organization is only as strong as its weakest link!

Your Mindset Matters

Another key to success is maintaining the proper mindset, one that only sees success and not failure, wealth and not poverty. I really went through some challenges in my journey to overcome negative emotions and poor self-esteem as it relates to achieving my business goals. Since I came from a background of sheer poverty, I felt deep inside that I would not be able to experience anything different. I couldn't clearly see that I was capable, little ole' me, of being a success story. I felt that no matter what I did, I would always, somehow remain poor.

This poverty mentality directly affected my ability to progress in life and achieve my career goals. The book of Proverbs, also known as the book of wisdom, tells us, "As a man thinks in his heart, so is he". This includes women. Basically, it says that you will never become more than you see yourself becoming. You first have to think or envision yourself and life and to the same degree that you develop your vision, you'll develop your life to match it.

The name of one of my businesses is eN'vision Hair Salon. The entire business foundation was built upon the concept of "envisioning my dreams" then using faith and work to see them realized. My dreams did not come easily, I had to fight for them, and you will have to fight for yours.

Have you heard the saying that anything worth having is worth fighting for? I can attest to that adage. The battles I faced were mostly internal, against the fear of failure, fear of the unknown, and fear of taking a road less traveled…following my own path in faith.

As I fought the good fight of faith, remaining dedicated to seeing my dreams realized despite intense internal opposition, I realized how important spirituality was. It's my belief that every earthly problem has a spiritual root and solution and both the root and solution can be found in the Bible. In seeking spiritual wisdom, I found the main cause of my battles. The root causes of most of the battles I faced in life were based in curses, generational curses. In short, generational curses are the effects of the "sins of our fathers". These are learned negative behaviors, mentalities, or "ways of being/living" that are continually passed down from one generation to the next. Generational curses are bondages (mental, physical, and emotional) that prevent people from moving freely into their destinies.

We have all been affected by generational curses at some level and in order for me to achieve success or live my dreams; I had to break free from the bondage in my mind.

The way I began to break and reverse spiritual curses in my life was through learning and applying the Word of God. A popular Bible verse says, "Once you know the truth, you will be made (become) free". We accept many things as truth because someone told us they were true, we have seen them on television, or through our life experiences, we have developed certain expectations. Unfortunately, life and people lie to us.

I had accepted that because I came from poverty I would always be poor. I assumed that because I did not see many examples of successful business owners in my neighborhood or on television, that it was hard or rare to be one. I had accepted that because I felt small, insecure, and inadequate, I was not capable of leading others in the market place. All of these were lies I had accepted in my life.

Once I began to dig into the Word of God, I learned the truth about my capabilities, and myself, then I became free to live my dreams! I learned that once I identified with and accepted the power of God within me, there was absolutely nothing I could not do. Once I began to feed my spirit man, the truth or the Word of God, I began to feel my faith increase. The Word gave me the capacity to disconnect from the old ways of thinking that limited me and the negative thought patterns that kept me in bondage. I saw that God's plan for my life was to prosper me and to help me realize my dreams. After all, He put them inside me for a reason, for me to fulfill a purpose on earth.

Your Pain is Connected to Your Purpose

My journey has taken me to several different places in life and not all of those places were positive. I remember going through a long period of depression when I was 25 years old. I had just moved to Atlanta after having lost my mom and experiencing divorce. Things were moving along on the outside; I was going through the motions enough to get by, but I was stuck on the inside. For almost two years, I prayed to God that He would not wake me up. I was a young mother and I would take my sons to school, then go home and get in the bed. My prayer to God was consistent, "Don't wake me up".

At the time, I was in the church; around many other people, helping them, pressing and praying for them, but no one knew the pain I was in. No one seemed to be able to see through my mask to the pain that was inside me. Although I was trying to help everyone else, no one reached out to help me. All the people I trusted and depended on had expired. I did not understand why none of these "spiritual people" could sense that I needed help. This made me bitter and I began to feel that church people were fake. I put up a barrier and wouldn't make close relationships with people because I was scared everyone I got close to would leave me. I felt the church people did not understand what I was going through nor did they try to connect with me and my needs while I was a part of their congregation. For some reason, I just felt like they should have been able to hear my silent scream for help, but they didn't.

God Answers our Prayers

Some people say you should not question God, but I did, a lot. I learned that it was ok to consult with God. He is a friend who wants to be involved in assisting me with every part of my life. In response to a prayer, God placed two young people in my path that helped me to get through that dark season. They showed me an example of having a solid relationship with God and how from this relationship, all other things can flow in your life like joy, peace, love, and success in all areas.

It was my usual custom to associate with older women, because they gave me a lot of wisdom, but this time the ladies who helped me were younger than me. God used one of them to give me a book, *Why*, by TD Jakes. After receiving the book, I knew God was using it to speak directly to me. I felt it all over. I took some personal time to read the book, spend alone with God and get an understanding from His perspective as to why I was in so much pain and why I felt disconnected and stuck. He answered all of the questions and my friendship with God grew from this point.

The depression miraculously broke. I had a breakthrough experience while reading God's Word in the book given to me. From that day forward, I began protecting my environment, disconnecting from negativity and feeding myself the Word daily to strengthen my faith.

My heart for prayer was birthed from the healing experience that began with me reading the TD Jakes book a friend gave me in the salon. Prayer is a powerful way to launch yourself into your destiny, if your intent and desires are pure. It goes back to the principle of giving and receiving. When you sacrificially give of yourself and your time, to desire the best for someone else and to place the needs of others before your own in prayer, it sets in motion the principle of reciprocity. Before you know it, your own needs are being met by others that God will place in your path specifically to help you along the way. No matter what you set out to achieve in life, keeping a pure heart that considers the needs of others first, will always lead to personal freedom and success in your life.

Once the depression lifted, my vision for life began to get a bit clearer. I started to have hope and dream again. God continued to place people in my path to help me get over hurdles so I could arrive at the next destination on my journey.

One of these special persons was Gloria Johnson, a client, who invited me to her church the Love Center. There, I met Stephanie Cooksey, also a client who gave me another TD Jakes book, Woman Thou Art Loosed. Both of these ladies were godly ladies who lived a life of faith. The book impacted me so much I wrote a letter to Bishop Jakes after reading it just to thank him for the ministry. During this time, I was still learning how to maintain my freedom, not regress and go back into a place of mental bondage. I took advantage of grief and loss counseling offered at The Love Center.

Byron L. Broussard, the Pastor of the church, also became a client and I gained much wisdom from our time together. I would pick his brain about spiritual things and about life. I asked him many questions most people would probably feel uncomfortable asking their clergy. My position is if you never ask, then how will you get an answer?

This perspective as an entrepreneur and business owner has always placed me ahead of the game and given me an advantage over the competition. I'm not afraid to ask questions, I take advantage of the knowledge resources around me, and then I use that information to solve personal issues.

I loved how he would respond to my questions that would often challenge the status quo or traditional beliefs within the Christian community. He would give me open-ended answers based on the Word, which forced me to seek out more knowledge for myself through studying, so that I could come to my own conclusion. At the end of the day, we are all on a journey and must follow our own path. While guidance from others is a helpful start, ultimately, we must dedicate time to our own personal development through research and study as a means to prepare for destiny.

It was amazing to see how my previous negative feelings about the church and "church folks" changed during this phase of my life. God just kept sending me special people, who happened to also be in the church, to love on me, personally nurture me, to help me heal and to model godliness. Bernice King, Martin Luther King, Jr.'s youngest daughter, was one of these persons. She was the associate Pastor at The Love Center. She loved ministry and growing and developing people. She taught me about the struggles she experienced growing up as the daughter of a Civil Rights leader. How she too came from poverty but disconnected from the generational curses that attempted to hold her hostage. She deposited so much wisdom and life experience into the ladies of the church. She naturally wanted to share her life as a means to assist others in their journeys. Just hearing some of the horrible things she and her family went through and overcame during the Civil Rights period showed me there was no reason for me to ever give up. Her testimony of victory over so many obstacles inspired me to go harder, to live louder, and to always know that if God saw her through every adversity she faced, He also would do the same for me. Her life motivated me to go after my dreams with a vengeance, to really live and make a difference and impact the world. She taught me the way to do all of these things was to pursue my passions.

Pursue your passions...not a paycheck.

"Don't waste time going through the motions working a job that you hate." When I advise clients, students, or participants in my business seminars or workshops to pursue their passions, I usually get the response, "I don't know what my passions are".

When I work with a new client seeking to discover their life motivations or passions, the first thing we talk about is the concept of lifestyle design. I ask them, "What do you want your life to look like?" If you were to design a business without answering this question, you could create a nice, profitable venture that is completely incompatible with your life goals. You'd most likely make money, but you'd probably be miserable.

I will generally use 'passions' and 'purpose' interchangeably as they usually go hand in hand. To find your life purpose, lifestyle design isn't necessarily a crucial component. However, since we're talking about entrepreneurial purpose, lifestyle design is indeed crucial in building a business that you'll enjoy and remain passionate about.

For example, if your desire is to spend more time at home with your family. Would you be happy with a business that kept you in an office long hours or out of town most of the time? On the flip side, if your desire was to travel and see the world, you wouldn't be able to do that if your business required your presence, day in and day out, to survive.

So, the concept of Life Design will aid you in creating a clear vision for yourself, your family, and your business, as all of these things are connected and affect each other. We will start by getting some clarity on your personal goals and spending time working on designing your life.

Basically, Life Designing is creating a vision. Since most people need a little prodding in order to understand their true desires which is necessary in creating a life design or vision, many people from all professional backgrounds and life experiences hire me to coach or mentor them to work through this process. Many people are used to the idea that there is a certain way life "should" be. On the contrary, there is no specific way life should or shouldn't be. The sky is the limit and you have the freedom to create the life you want. In order to do that, you must first realize that the power is in your hands.

Below are a more steps that will assist you in the process of Life Designing or beginning to create a vision for your life and business:

1. Give yourself permission to dream. Keep in mind that this is your life and you can live it any way you choose. All of your dreams are only a decision away. Some may call it fantasizing, but let your imagination run here. To pull out your true dreams, answer this question: "If you had no fears or financial limitations, what would your ideal life look like? What would you do with your time to feel totally content and happy?

2. Once you've figured out your lifestyle design, create a vision, we will do a bit more soul-searching to figure out what you're truly passionate about. This process requires you to review and evaluate your life, to really look within and look back. Specifically, look back over your life history to find out, "When you were the happiest and what have you enjoyed doing the most?"

Remember when attempting to identify your passions, what you are looking for doesn't necessarily have to be an actual past or current job in its entirety, but can possibly be certain aspects of past jobs or hobbies that you've really enjoyed, that have inspired or motivated you.

Think about the bigger picture, your life purpose. Many successful entrepreneurs have earned their place in history by setting out to make an impact on the world. They have a core desire to make a difference. Is there a specific issue or cause that is important to you? Is there a problem that you would like to help find a solution for?

For some, this process of passion discovery comes easily. Generally, once a person begins to answer these types of vision-focused questions, the answers come quickly. For others, it may be more difficult. In some cases, people may suffer from a generalized lack of passion and purpose in life. This can come from having suppressed their passions for too long. Sometimes it can come from eating poorly and a lack of exercise. Occasionally, it may have something to do with their internal chemistry or programming. If the latter applies to you, it may be useful for you to seek help from a trained professional coach, mentor, or counselor.

In other cases, not knowing your true purpose may just be a matter of not having discovered it yet.

If this is the case, now is the time to explore! The Internet is a great tool for learning and exploration, begin this journey by searching for hobbies and careers and learn as much as you can about any topic that triggers your interest. Once you have done this, follow up at the library on the top ten things that really intrigue you. Again, remember this is your life and only you can give yourself permission to explore all that is available to you.

Find Your Entrepreneurial Purpose.

I've shared with you when and how I knew that I had discovered my own, it kind of hit me like a ton of bricks. While working at McDonald's during my youth, I just decided I would no longer be an employee of another person. I resolved within myself I could and would be a business owner. That's not to say I found success immediately after that moment. But rather, the path ahead of me was clear, so I knew what to do. Follow my inner voice that told me that I could and would own my own business. Since I have always loved the beauty industry, styling hair, applying make-up, and training others in the art of fashion production, I had an indication of what my passions were. This knowledge helped me to choose jobs and make career choices that allowed me to work in the area of my passions. Even though I did not always know how all of it would come together professionally, I knew what I wanted to do with my life. By knowing exactly what you want, you are more likely to get what you want. This is my story, my experience. In essence, I designed success for myself, not by what others felt I should do to be "successful" or "happy".

You really can create success on your own terms, according to your own definition of what success means to you. Dig deep, look within, and seek whatever help you need to honestly put all of your true-life desires, dreams, and visions on the table. It starts with identifying the things in life that motivate you, inspire you, and bring you joy. The things that make your heart beat faster are generally your passions, Doing the things that you were created to do. Once you find that purpose and passion, your life, not just your entrepreneurial life, but your entire life, will never be the same. You will find that you will no longer have to chase money or paychecks, but your life mission will be to run after your dreams and fulfill your life assignment through your career choices. Once you are firmly on this path of purpose, money will naturally follow you. I am a witness.

Pursue your passions...not a paycheck.

Nothing great in the world has ever
been accomplished without passion.
- Georg Wilhelm Friedrich Hegel

I am sure you are asking, "What does pursuing your passion mean?" People talk about it all the time, but what does it *really* mean? Does it mean quitting your 9 - 5 and turning your love of photography, dance or food into your career?

My answer would be, possibly. It's very important for everyone to follow their passions and do what they feel inspired to do, but that doesn't necessarily mean turning it into a business. Maybe you like your day job, or you need the health benefits. If this is the case, keep your job, but make sure you have some inspirational passion infused in your life at least as a part-time job or gift to the world through volunteerism.

If you really want to be happy, follow your passion. Following your passion for work or a hobby, helps you tap into your gifts and talents. The act of following your passion allows you to become comfortable with skills in areas you're already strong in and pushes you to become better. Then you are ready to share them with the world. In this way, you begin to create a body of work that will grow and develop over your lifetime.

Some people may not be ready to pursue their passion just yet, for a career that is uncertain at best. If you're familiar with Maslow's Hierarchy of Needs then you know there are basic needs that must be addressed before you can move forward with your passion. The basic needs are food, shelter, safety, love, friendship etc. Once your basic needs are met, you are ready to move up the pyramid and eventually reach the pinnacle of "self-actualization" or operating at your highest level. Our highest need is to be creative, but most of the time; we get stuck in meeting our basic need for food, water, shelter etc. This keeps us in "survival mode" as opposed to becoming the greatest version of ourselves.

I have included a sample diagram of Maslow's Hierarchy of Needs for your review. The diagram will assist you in understanding human needs and related thought processes that may affect and keep you from taking a leap into the deep to pursue your dreams. Our focus however, will be on why you should base your goals on the hierarchy of needs.

ABRAHAM MASLOW
HIERARCHY OF NEEDS

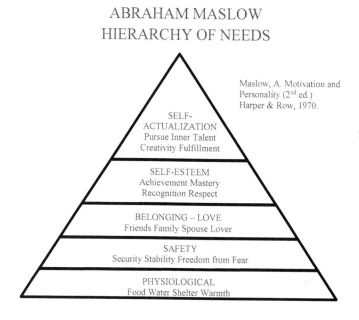

Maslow, A. Motivation and Personality (2nd ed.) Harper & Row, 1970.

SELF-ACTUALIZATION
Pursue Inner Talent
Creativity Fulfillment

SELF-ESTEEM
Achievement Mastery
Recognition Respect

BELONGING – LOVE
Friends Family Spouse Lover

SAFETY
Security Stability Freedom from Fear

PHYSIOLOGICAL
Food Water Shelter Warmth

Feeling happiness and fulfillment – When you use your time to value your talents, giving attention and resources to your passion, you will find a piece of the greatest bliss you could ever hope for. Some of us have childhood passions we gave up on, like skate boarding, cross-stitching or collecting vintage dresses. It is one thing to quit because you've lost your passion for it, but it is another to quit because what you love to do seems impractical for one reason or another. Although I do feel that once a person gets over fear and pursues their dreams with their whole heart, money will follow. If you choose to just do the things you love as a hobby, you still win because you cannot put a price on feeling happy or fulfilled as a person. That is also wealth. As such, it's my opinion it is always practical to nurture and develop your passion, whether you are paid or unpaid because it taps into your authentic self and grows that part of you.

Professional Development; Become an Expert – Taking the time to pursue your passion, will immediately sharpen your skills and gifts, which leads to developing an expertise. Don't you want to be an expert on something? As you develop your skills, more and more people will seek you out to advise them on your area of expertise. Becoming an expert in any given subject matter, directly leads to countless new opportunities to include moneymaking opportunities.

Don't Miss Out on Infinite Opportunities – The statement that there are infinite opportunities available, many that are created even when you work your areas of passion doesn't necessarily make everyone want to run out and quit their day jobs. By pursuing your passions, we don't mean jump out of the boat without a paddle or start a venture without a plan. This would mean acting on faith and adrenaline alone. I'm suggesting you strategically address your dreams, plan to live on purpose and plan to live your dreams. Smart business people plan, plan, and plan to succeed.

Below are a few reasons why some of us who have attempted to follow our dreams were met with disappointment:

No Strategy – Wishful thinking will not cut it. You have to understand exactly what doing meaningful work in the way you want will require of you, your family and your bank account. What it will require financially, emotionally and behaviorally. To make it work, you need a sound, well-developed business plan and/or strategic plan that covers the logistics of your vision or dream.

Lack of commitment – People who want to move out of their careers into something more satisfying or desire to start a business of their own often don't realize how long it will take, and how much effort it requires. If you really want this, you have to work at it, and work long and hard. The thing is, if you are doing what you're passionate about, it won't feel like "hard work" – it will feel exciting, exhilarating, and life affirming.

Unclear mission & purpose – This is an important concept to grasp if you want to be successful doing passion-filled work. First, you have to figure out the essence of what you want, the purpose of the work, the outcome you want to deliver, the legacy you want to leave, the energy behind it, and the feelings you'll experience doing it.

I spoke earlier about having the proper mind-set and intent when seeking to do anything. For instance, just because you love volunteering with kids doesn't mean you'll love teaching full-time in a public school. If you love singing, that doesn't mean you'll love earning a living singing at your friends' weddings or cocktail parties. You can use your passions and talents many ways in the world, you need to identify the right expressions for that passion then properly identify your desired outcomes from making this life change. For example, by opening a new group home, I yearn to provide hope and job opportunities to underrepresented populations. I aim to provide a stable and loving home for at-risk youth in transition, reducing the number of homeless children and decreasing the dropout rates in my state.

Poor money management skills – Most of us weren't taught how to manage money effectively. To be financially successful, you have to respect and appreciate money, but not for money's sake. You have to respect it for what it can do and offer in the world. Basically, you must see it as a tool for the betterment of others. Selfish desires will ruin a great business. Failure to enlist adequate professional assistance such as accountants, budgeting specialist, or financial counselors is a recipe for disaster. These team members are a necessary-part of the goal.

Self-sabotaging – Some people want success, but somehow feel they just don't deserve it. They feel that success, accomplishing their professional goals, making it big or living life according to their own terms is okay for others but not for them. It's almost as if they feel that making money in this area feels wrong or dirty, so they cut themselves off at the knees. For example, you are highly skilled at teaching piano and people come from near and far to learn from you, but you feel guilty charging for your services. I see this happening a lot with friends or people who attend the same church. People do not want to charge clients in these categories for services provided.

There are times when you may want to give services free or barter with another person service for service and that is absolutely fine, but you cannot do this continuously and expect to make money. Your time and skills are valuable; you must believe that and charge competitive rates for the services you bring to the market place.

Poor communication of expectations and boundaries – You can't make great money drawing on your passions if you have weak boundaries and can't speak up. To be successful in business and professional endeavors, you must communicate powerfully, engender support, build helpful relationships, and be a powerful advocate and negotiator for what you need and want. Exhibiting weakness and insecurity means you won't successfully move forward doing this work, and you'll fail to deliver the outcomes, in your own life and in the world for which you long.

We have addressed a few blockers that keep us from tapping into our passions. For those who chose to break past the blockers and begin our journey to starting a new career, launching a new business, or working directly in our area of passion, we have also looked at some misguided ways of thinking that knock us off course after we have gotten started. Both of the above scenarios should cause us to evaluate our decisions, whatever they are, to see if we are on the right track. The evaluation pointers below will assist you in doing so before we proceed to the next section, which focuses on selecting a career path.

First, we want to make sure you have properly identified your true passion so you may build all other career-based decisions from that place. Here are a few ways to identify your TRUE passions:

- Remember what you loved to do as a child – Often; our truest passions emerged in childhood, only to be smothered by "real life" pressures. So think back and recall what you loved long before you had to worry about actually finding a career. Was it writing poetry, doing scientific experiments or taking care of people? Getting back in touch with those instincts is an important step in finding your true passion.

- Eliminate money from the equation – Mindset matters and we have to begin to think about the possibilities instead of the perceived restrictions. If money were no object, what would you do with your life? Would you travel? Would you spend all of your time with your children? Would you start a charitable organization to help abused women? Of course money can't be ignored, but don't let financial pressures dictate your choices. It seems like a "Catch 22", your career should ultimately lead to financial security, but if financial security is the defining motivator, it's unlikely you'll end up doing what you love.

- Get feedback from family and friends – Sometimes you're not the best judge of what makes you happy. Ask the people who know you intimately when you seemed to be the happiest and what you do the most enthusiastically. Their answers may surprise you.
- Research Career Paths in University Catalogs
- Find some quiet time and look through career catalogs to see which courses naturally interest you. If you were given free tuition to a school of your choice, what courses would you take? If not to

study, what courses do you think you could teach others? Which subjects scare you out of your mind, and which ones do you find boring? Revisiting these possibilities will help point you in the direction of subjects and topics you love and career paths that are "for you".

- Identify a Professional Role Model – Of everyone you know, either personally or in your extended frame of reference (from your dentist to Oprah), whose career would you most like to emulate? Reach out to them to learn more about how they got to where they are. If that's not possible, for inspiration and direction for your own journey, read about how they chose their career path and the challenges they overcame. Sometimes, it's best not to reinvent the wheel, but follow the advice of those who have achieved great success and use their blueprint as a road map to where we want to go. Work smarter not harder.

Get Started

Once you have a solid idea of what you love doing, it can still be a big leap to turn that passion into a viable career. Here are four easy steps to start making the transition:

1. Consult with a Career Counselor or Business Mentor – Career counselors help others figure out what they want to do for a living, and they'll have insights and tools to help you zero in on the things you love most and naturally do best. They also may be able to offer ideas and guidance on how to find a career that best compliments or supports your passions.

   Identifying a person who is currently working in the ideal career path or business you desire is most helpful in assisting you to work in your own. They have walked the path, overcome challenges and understand the journey. It is wise to listen to, follow their advice and take advantage of these basic resources.

2. Leverage Social Media – The Internet is our friend; it contains so much information and affords us unlimited

opportunities to learn about whatever we want to do. Once you've identified what it is you love, use Facebook, Twitter, and LinkedIn to connect with people who share your areas of interest. Read blogs, join forums and networks. Sometimes there are business opportunities just waiting for you to connect online. Attend events that will allow you to meet your mentors, learn directly from those whom you admire, and learn "secrets to their success" by simply being at the right place at the right time.

3. Start saving money – Once you feel strongly that you want to start down a new career path, or feel you may want to open a new business in the near future, start saving your money. The more money you have in the bank, the less finances will influence your decision to continue following your dreams.

4. Just do it – Ultimately, you won't really know what you love to do unless you actually bite the bullet and try it out. Just do it! If it works out great, if it doesn't, that's ok too. The important thing is that

you tried. You'll have learned key pieces of information about yourself, your likes, dislikes, and essential professional needs. You will have had a taste of doing something that you really love. If it is really a passion, you won't be able to easily stop doing it, even if you don't make money at it at first.

I found my passion—and I'm grateful for that. But these tips still serve me well as I go down my path of business growth and expansion, because it's important that my work continue to be fueled by what I love most. As you delve deeper into that vein, finding out what you love and doing it, you will also have to continue to prioritize the things that are most important to you and this will keep you feeling fulfilled, alive, and happy.

Signs You Are on the Right Career Path

Just as signs of happiness, fulfillment, and joy are general indicators you are on the right path, feeling unhappy, unfulfilled, and "void of life" are equal indicators you may be on a path that is not necessarily for you.

There will be times in our lives when we don't feel like we are on cloud nine, but I'm not saying that because you don't feel exceptionally exhilarated every day in your profession that you are on the wrong path. What I am saying however, is when you are truly on the path that is for you, you will feel a certain level of inner peace and joy for life. You will jump out of bed each morning with excitement and anticipation about what the day has in store. You'll look forward to doing what you do.

The truth is, we all have the potential to do something amazing. We all possess an intense, passionate, and thoughtful self within us. And we all deserve to wake up motivated and fall asleep fulfilled because we are fearlessly giving that self to the world, by doing something we love.

Our feelings can sometimes be viewed as our internal guidance system as we travel through life. As such, if feelings of joy, motivation, inspiration and professional exhilaration are signs that we are on the right path, then let's look at the other side of the coin to outline a few signs that we may be going down the wrong path and need a change of direction. Here are five signs you should change career paths:

1. Feelings of chronic fatigue, exhaustion or depletion – To find the root cause of chronic illness, debilitation, and exhaustion, the first place to look is your work. Most of us spend more waking hours working than anything else, and I can tell you from firsthand experience that if you don't like your work, it won't like you back, and overly-stressful, misaligned work can very easily make your body break down. As I stated before, our feelings are a part of our internal guidance system. *Your body tells you what your lips or mind cannot.* It may be your specific job or a toxic work environment that is breaking you down. The signs are trying to tell you that your entire career may need a shift.

2. Your skills, responsibilities, and tasks don't reflect your inner desires – This can be a shocker for some people, the fact that you might have become very good at work you hate. I excelled at presenting facts, data and new marketing strategies about the membership products I managed to a boardroom of senior leaders, but inside

me, it was a horrible struggle. I just couldn't seem to hold on to the key statistics or data about these products because I couldn't care less about them.

3. Your salary no longer compensates for feelings of boredom and emptiness – I've coached many people who dislike their work but are reluctant to make a change because of the fear of losing their "financial security". The reality is, there is no real financial security when you work for someone else. Even if the company is strong, stable, and growing, at any moment things could change. The company could shut down, move, or downsize without notice to you. With this in mind, it just behooves us all to be in the mindset of "thinking outside of the box" and begin to access additional forms of income using resources we already possess, our gifts and talents.

4. Despite making all of the "right choices" in your career, the outcome feels wrong – This deals with doing some soul-searching to identify the things you wish to experience in life. This is separate from

what others feel you should do. So many people have made all the "right" choices; they have done everything that was expected of them by their families. So, when they wake up bored to no end with their work, they're shocked and completely confused. The thing to realize here is that the "right" choices usually had to do with pleasing others or taking work or a promotion that fell in your lap, rather than asking yourself the tough questions like "Is this where I belong right now?" "Am I using my gifts and talents to fulfill my purpose?

5. Feeling your talents and abilities could or should be used in a totally different (more creative and impactful) way – This feeling is generally expressed in levels and people choose not to move on the urgency for change because:

Level 1: The job pays the bills and you receive benefits.

Level 2: You enjoy the work you do at some level and the people you work with. Basically, you are comfortable and don't want to rock the boat.

Level 3: You believe you are contributing to something important. You're aligned with a mission, and your actions and hard work have a purpose larger than yourself.

We know the higher the level of connection, the greater your resilience, which means you're far more able to weather the storm, to cope with stress and bear up under tough times. In fact, the more engaged and connected you are to the company's goals the more fulfilled you will be as a person because you truly believe in what you are doing every day, its purpose. This is the only reason I would say you should continue to work in the area you are in and maybe search for other outlets or expressions of the job you are doing. Maybe it is the right field or area, because you actually feel fulfilled, but it's time for you to expand your knowledge base in another location...maybe in your own establishment.

If you are still unclear if you are on the right career path or if the work you are doing or wish to do is right for you, the evaluation list below will help you gain more clarity.

Get a pen and sheet of paper and respond to the questions below with "Often", "Sometimes", "Rarely" or "Never" for each question.

1. I get excited every morning when I get out of bed to prepare for work.
2. I feel accomplished when I think of what I do for a living.
3. I feel overwhelmed with gratitude about my life and profession.
4. My life feels like a grand adventure.
5. I have fun at my job and I generally enjoy doing my work.
6. Things just seem to work out well for me overall.
7. I do things I love on a daily basis.
8. I feel on top of my game professionally.
9. I get so involved in my work projects that I lose track of time.
10. People seem to enjoy being around me.
11. I do what I deeply want to do, even if it's scary.
12. I have great ideas and I use them in my profession.
13. I feel so much love for other people.
14. I use my imagination at work and my creative ideas are appreciated.

15.I feel deeply understood.

Now, tally your answers. If you answered, "rarely" and "never" more often than "sometimes" this would generally indicate you might be on the wrong path and in need of a career change.

YOU CAN MAKE MONEY DOING WHAT YOU LOVE

Ok. So you have evaluated your current professional situation and have a good understanding of whether you are on the right path or if you may be in need of a career change. One main hindrance for many of us taking the next step once we realize a career change may be needed is the fear we can't make "good money" doing what we love to do. That is completely untrue!

It's painful to sit behind a desk inside a walled office when your soul longs to be free to do something creative, meaningful, and exciting. It longs to use its unique talents and experiences to positively impact the world. The good news is, it's perfectly natural to desire the aforementioned and you can get paid well, while experiencing your soul's desires.

Some of us have been thinking about this for years, but haven't taken action because of FEAR. The key is learning to push past fear. So how do you do that? A few suggestions would be to make time for mindful practices that support cleaning your brain from old ways of thinking so that you may adopt a new way of thinking. Prayer, Yoga, listening to and repeating positive affirmations or mantras are very useful in this process of training your brain to be positive and optimistic. You must download faith-filled words into your vocabulary and thought processes and uproot fear-centered thinking completely.

At the same time, taking small steps in the direction of your dreams, doing your research, creating a vision board, or going back to school if necessary to support your dream, will also increase your confidence and help uproot fear. Sometimes just doing something related to realizing your dream will show you that you are capable and the whole process was not as hard as you thought. Step out of your comfort zone every day in small and large ways; this is a mental exercise! It grows your faith in yourself and your abilities to accomplish your goals.

Find a support system. It doesn't have to be family or even friends, just people with a similar mindset that also believe in what you are doing. Surround yourself with progressive, driven, and creative people. The reality is you are the sum average of the people with whom you spend most time. If you desire to be a successful entrepreneur, begin to surround yourself with them!

I can't say that you will "feel ready" to launch out. The idea is that because you believe so much in the importance of living your dreams and fulfilling your purpose here on earth, you start "doing it" in faith, sometimes before you actually feel ready. Start *before* you're ready.

Finding your purpose in the world is much less about "figuring it out" and more about letting it "emerge from your soul." Many of the clients I coach tell me that before we started working together, they had spent many years trying to figure out what their passion and purpose was. As a result, they usually changed jobs every couple of years with hopes that the next one would fill the void. Unfortunately, it usually didn't. This pattern tends to repeat itself until they finally do what they are here on earth to do. This is why spending a reasonable amount of time learning who you are, what gifts you have to give the world and locating your passions will lead you directly to your purpose. This in turn, will alleviate all of the guesswork and immediately place you on the right path not only professionally, but also for life.

I've also suggested you use a notebook or journal while reading this book. Recording your thoughts and writing the creative ideas and visions provoked by this book will be direct signs that lead you to living a life of passion and purpose.

Spending time thinking about and doing activities you love will help you deepen your heart space, the space of your soul. When you spend more time there, your offering to the world unfolds with ease.

So How Do I Make Money Doing What I Love?

I have a friend that makes around half a million dollars a year...teaching yoga. When most people find this out, they say, "OMG, I wish I could make that much doing what I love!"

Although we explore this in detail during our business seminars, workshops and conferences, I will share a few practical ways to make money doing what you love.

My friend didn't make over $500,000 teaching Yoga with anything special, besides her natural interest in helping others. She did not have money, training, or any special "know how" to start a business. She did however, have a corporate job that she hated, and a sense of urgency that she should put some energy towards living her dreams.

Although it took her over seven years to achieve the $500,000 mark, that is still quite an accomplishment. When you consider she did not have any business mentors or books like the one you are reading now to steer her in the right direction and prevent her from making mistakes that could have been prevented by having a few key pieces of wisdom before she started teaching.

She often tells the classrooms of students she teaches on entrepreneurships that she probably could have met that same financial goal within a year or two by just having read material on understanding how fulfilling your purpose in life will lead you to financial prosperity and learning the importance of getting beyond the fear of failure. She admits that she would have moved a lot more swiftly towards what she felt in her heart if she had more confidence initially. That her confidence came by intuitively jumping into doing something she had a little "urge" to do. Her gut told her she should try teaching a class in Yoga because she had practiced it for years out of pure enjoyment and knew a lot about the art. Little did she know many other people in the world were waiting for her to offer her services so they could benefit. There was a demand for her natural abilities and by following her urge, she went from living paycheck to paycheck to making half a million dollars in her spare time doing what she absolutely loved to do. You can do the same.

If you dive into these application steps, you'll be much closer to beginning your journey to tapping into your multi-million streams of income. You will turn your work hours into very profitable life's work.

Make sure your notebook is nearby so you can give each of the points serious thought. Brainstorm about them and write down any action steps that jump out at you. The statements that seem to "jump out at you" are signs you may want to pay special attention to as a starting point for the next phase of your journey as it relates to this topic.

Destroy the Walls

When it comes to living your dreams, you can be your own best friend or your worst enemy. There is no competition for your special path in life, only you getting in or out of your own way helps you to win 1st place. Stop listening to the negative voices, outside or inside, that tell you, "You can't." Start saying, "I can, watch me".

Don't wait. I believe procrastination is the slow death of many dreams. If you wait for the stars to align before you start doing what you feel in your heart you are meant to do, you'll be waiting forever. Even the tiniest steps propel you forward toward realizing your dream. Start now.

You are responsible for creating your next opportunity. Since most people wait for other people to give them opportunities, I want you to take control, and Do It Yourself. Create the opportunity you want. I don't just follow dreams. Like my friend who followed her intuition to begin teaching a Yoga class and ended up making a half million dollars, she created her opportunity as opposed to waiting to be hired as a Yoga instructor by someone else.

Don't be afraid to ask for what you're worth. I've seen an unfortunate epidemic amongst indie creators: they take the term "starving artist" to heart and sometimes do not charge people for their services out of compassion. The reality is, in the market place and life in general, people take things more seriously which they perceive to have a higher value. Your price tag should make you feel slightly giddy but still be within your target market's budget or competitive price range. It all begins with knowing your worth. Once you do, you won't feel bad about placing the proper value on the services you provide.

ENTREPRENEURS 101

ENTREPRENEURS USE THE POWER OF

VISION

From my perspective, every successful business or businessperson has a successful mindset. Their thoughts are rooted in having a strong mental image for their life.

Basically, I'm saying all successful people have a clear vision for their lives; they have painted a picture in their minds of who they desire to be, where they wish to go and what they want to do when they get there. After seeing the picture of all they wish to accomplish in their minds, they make a plan to execute, then they execute. Pretty simple huh? Yes, it's a simple concept, but the application tends to get a lot of us stuck from time to time.

This chapter addresses the importance of having a clear life vision and how to apply it to accomplish your personal and professional goals.

I believe we all are entrepreneurs, if we choose to be. Anything we want to be or do is just a vision and decision away. An entrepreneur is a person who sees an opportunity, makes a plan, organizes and manages the undertaking, assumes the risk for the sake of profit, then receives the profit.

In the previous pages, we were encouraged to look within and really find out what we are passionate about and begin, at some level to do it. We were also inspired to believe that our dreams of making a career of doing what we love can in fact become a reality. When we have an accurate belief system in place, we are capable of accomplishing anything we set our minds to, our visions are able to come alive and move forward.

Driving the Vehicles of Success; Using our Gifts & Talents

I believe each person has natural gifts inside them, that if utilized strategically, they can be very successful making money doing the things that come naturally to them. In other words, we all have a business or two or three inside us, we just have to learn to pull them out and make them work for us. When we use our gifts and talents in faith to support our visions, they grow. Consequently, so will more creative ideas, opportunities to apply the ideas, and potential profits from doing what you love to do.

To create an extraordinary quality of life, you must create a vision that's not only obtainable, but that is sustainable.

Anthony Robbins

Achieving "success" in life, however you envision success, is rooted in having an overall vision of how you would like to live your life, spend your time, and use your personal assets, which are your gifts, talents, and professional skills. Creating a life vision might seem like a frivolous and fantastic waste of time, but it's not: developing a compelling picture of the life you REALLY want is actually one of the most effective strategies for obtaining it.

The best way to look at the concept of a life vision is by comparing it to having a compass or guide, to help you move in the direction of your true intentions; having a map to keep you focused on taking the necessary steps that will propel you toward living your best life.

For this reason, creating a life vision is not just something fun to do or something to do if you have time; you NEED a life vision. If you are serious about obtaining what you want, it is a necessary part of your career planning. No matter who you ask, if they are successful in life, meaning they have achieved their personal or professional goals or are "living their dreams" they will tell you the same. They will attest that having a clear vision was one of the major factors contributing to their success. They had an end destination in mind, visualized and researched various paths to arrive there, used the signs along the road in their journey that directed or guided them in their travels, and they got there!

The harsh reality is if you don't develop your own vision, you allow other people and circumstances to direct the course of your life. I'm not saying that once you start this process, you should expect to have a well-defined vision overnight, envisioning your life and determining the course you will follow requires time and a lot of reflection. You must cultivate vision, perspective, and apply logical planning for the practical application of your vision.

Your vision blossoms from areas of passion, your dreams, hopes, and aspirations. It will resonate with your values and ideas, and generate energy and enthusiasm to help strengthen your commitment to explore the infinite possibilities of your life.

What do you want? I mean what do you REALLY want? The question sounds deceptively simple, but it's often one of the most difficult to answer. We touched on this earlier in the book, but allowing yourself to explore your deepest desires can be very frightening. When we think about doing things we have not done before, it can sometimes make us uncomfortable. You may also think you don't have the time to consider something as fanciful as what you want out of life, but it's important to remind yourself that a life of fulfillment does not usually happen by chance, it happens by design.

You can start the life visioning process by asking yourself some thought-provoking questions to help you discover the possibilities of what you want out of life. You will need your note pad again as we go a little deeper in this area mentioned earlier in the book under the section EMBRACE THE POSSIBILTIIES.

You want to consider every aspect of your life, personal and professional, tangible and intangible. Contemplate all the important areas, family and friends, career success, health and quality of life, spiritual connection, personal growth, and don't forget about fun and enjoyment!

Here are a few tips to guide you as you enVISION living your best life:

- Think about what you do want, not only what you don't want.
- What are your values? What issues do you care about?
- Why do you want the things you want? (i.e. more money?)
- Give yourself permission to dream BIG.
- Be creative. Consider ideas you never thought possible (for you).
- Focus on your truest desires, not what others expect of you.
- Decide what you would like to have more of in your life.
- Setting aside money for a moment, exactly what do you want to happen with your career?
- Write down your secret passions and dreams (again even if you did this earlier. This time be more descriptive or add new ideas).
- What would bring more joy and happiness to your life right now?
- What would your ideal relationships be like with your family? Friends? Spouse? Significant other? Romantic Interest?

- What personal and professional qualities would you like to develop?
- What would you most like to accomplish?
- What are your identified gifts and talents? What is special about you?
- What kind of legacy would you like to leave behind?

Add your own questions, and then ask others what they want out of life to get your creative juices flowing. Relax and let this exercise be fun. You may want to set your answers aside for a while and come back to them later to see if any have changed or if you have anything to add after finishing this book or doing more career research in the area of your passion.

Describe your ideal life vision in detail. Be free to dream, imagine, and create a vivid picture in your mind. If you can't visualize a mental picture, focus on how your best life would feel if you were already living it. If you find it hard to envision your life 10 or 20 years from now, start with just two or three years in the future. As you set aside any preconceived notions about what you can and can't have or do, you'll be amazed at the things you come up with. This is your chance to dream and fantasize.

Let's continue envisioning our best life by thinking from a place of having already acquired the things we desire. Now that you are living your dreams:

- What are you most proud of having accomplished?
- How will you feel about yourself as a successful __ (you fill in the blank)?
- What kind of people are in your life? How do you feel about them?
- What does your ideal day look like? How do you spend your time?
- Where do you live? Think specifics, what city, state, and country, type of community, house or apartment, style and atmosphere.
- What or who is your family comprised of? New significant other? Babies? Pets? A group of people or are you by yourself?
- How are you dressed? Where do you shop?
- What is your state of mind? Happy or sad? Content or frustrated?
- What does your physical body look like? How do you feel about that?

Thinking about living your best life should make you smile and make your heart happy. If it doesn't, dig deeper, dream BIGGER. It is important to focus on the results, the outcome, or the destination. Don't think so much about the process for getting there just yet—that's the next step. Revisit your vision every day, even if only for a few moments. Keep your vision alive by keeping it at the forefront and talking about it if only to yourself.

The next step is to plan backwards. It may sound counter-intuitive to plan backwards rather than forward, but when planning your life starting with the destination, it is often more useful to consider the last step and work your way back to the first. This is a valuable and practical strategy for making your vision a reality.

Let's think about some of the things that would've had to happen for you to achieve your best life. This process will help you locate deep thoughts, beliefs, and behaviors that may need to be addressed in order for you to live your best life.

Get a visual of your destination in mind; realizing your dreams. Imagine you have met all your career goals and are now living your best life. Now, think about where you are currently, as your read these pages, in relation to where you need to be to achieve your dreams. If you were to honestly consider the things that would have or could have hindered you from arriving at your end goal, what would they be? What changes were necessary along the way for you to be successful according to your life plan? Basically, what did you have to do to make your dreams come true?

This list of questions, are like a reflective interview for others attempting to follow your path after you have achieved your life goals. Answer them to the best of your ability and you'll receive inner guidance about things you may need to do right now to expedite your travel to destination success. Again, this is a mock reflective interview:

1. What was the most important choice you had to make in life to achieve your career goals?
2. What persons, places or things inspired you to believe that you were able to live your dreams?
3. What beliefs about yourself did you have to change in order to become so successful in business?
4. What habits or behaviors were hindrances to your progression?
5. What gifts, talents or skills did you have to cultivate to stand out and excel in your career field?

6. What type of support did you enlist? Friends Family? Spouse?
7. Who are your business role models and what did you learn from them about how to become successful?
8. What advice do you have for other who desire to live their dreams by changing career paths or starting a new business?

Good job. You may not see right now how this exercise provides you with inner guidance for your journey. But as you become more comfortable with visioning and experiencing the feelings of having arrived at your end destination, the place called success as opposed to "trying to get there" the more quickly you will become the person you envision in your mind.

We learn great wisdom keys from Scriptures, which tell us the importance of having a vision, documenting it in a clear fashion, and then following through with the plan. Proverbs 29:18 – "Without a vision, the people perish, but those that keep the law will be blessed". Habakkuk 2:2 – "Write the vision, and make it plain so that you and others may be able to accomplish the vision" (emphasis added). The first Scripture says that when we lack clear vision or revelation (revealed knowledge) about our lives, we run wild so to speak and are without restraint, which ultimately causes us to perish (the real us, the person we could be if we sought to live out our vision-inspired potential). The last part of the verse says, if we keep the law, we'll be happy; if we follow divine guidance and instructions based on laws of wisdom, blessings, or empowerment to prosper, we will be fulfilled in life.

God created the entire world from the vision He had in His mind. He said, "Let there be light, and there was light". There are many reasons why God our creator, who made us in his image, placed dreams and visions on the inside of us. He intended for us to see our internal visions, agree with them, by verbalizing or affirming them, then allowing the creation process to take place through our faith actions. He gave us big dreams and big visions because His goal is for us to affect the lives of many other people. He is a BIG GOD! His scope is so much larger than we can fathom, but we must enlarge our thinking to begin to align ourselves with His desires for us to do big things.

God's vision for your life includes you being happy, fulfilled, and blessed. He desires that you prosper personally and professionally and that by you living a creative, vision-led life, you'll reflect

His image as the ultimate Visionary and Divine Creator.

God has a vision for what He wants you to become and what He wants you to accomplish.

Our visions come from God, not some get-rich quick scheme or motivational speaker, but from God Himself. Philippians 4:13 encourages us to live a limitless life saying, "I can do ALL THINGS through and by God who empowers me!" Having that type of backup, God Himself on your side to support you, why not reach for the stars?

Continuing on the topic of life visioning will assist us as we move into the next area, which deals with further identifying and making career plans. Before we do that, I would like you to reflect for a moment on a few definitions of VISION:

- The ability to see in our mind, God's destination for our lives – this encompasses both the present and future.
- A mental blueprint for life.
- The eye of faith visualizes the invisible and decisiveness to make it visible.

- Adopting an action plan that enables you to do what God has shown you to do through enlightenment in service to Him.
- An inward fire that enables you to picture and communicate to others the future.
- An internal guidance system.
- The ability to sense God's presence, to perceive God's power, and to focus on God's plan in spite of challenges.
- Our capacity to allow God to creatively work through us by our use of natural gifts, talents, and skills that ultimately help others.

I have given you numerous definitions of vision and the necessity to adopt one that addresses all aspects of your life. We will begin to take action by supporting our visions with a plan.

Fully understanding the importance of having a strong, clear vision and actively working on a plan to bring it to fruition is essential. It is now time to revisit the topic of career planning.

CAREER PLANNING

Career planning is not an activity that should be done once in high school or college, and then left behind as we move forward in our jobs and careers. Rather, career planning is an ongoing activity that should be revisited on a regular basis. This is especially true given the data that the average worker will change careers (not jobs) multiple times over his or her lifetime. It's never too soon or too late to start or modify your career path.

Career planning is not a difficult activity, something to be dreaded or put off, but rather this activity should be liberating and fulfilling. It helps you access where you are in life in relation to where you desire to be, then aids you in identifying and taking the appropriate steps to achieve your goals. Whether you are at the beginning of your planning process, in transition or making minor adjustments towards the fulfillment of your dreams, career planning should be a rewarding and positive experience.

Review the following 10 tips to help you address visioning and planning for your ideal career path:

1. Conduct Annual Career Check-ups - Many of us have annual physicals, eye

exams and dental appointments, and do a myriad of other things regularly, so why not career planning? I would even tie it in as a part of my health check-up, because when we are not fulfilled in our career, when we are stressed or unhappy in general, it affects our overall health and wellbeing. By conducting career check-ups, we support our health goals. We all want to live healthy, wealthy, and prosperously in every area of our lives.

Find a day or weekend once a year to review and update your goals, more often if you feel the need, especially if you're planning a major career change. Simply schedule a retreat for yourself. Block out all distractions so you have the necessary time to reflect on your goals and focus on your current and future career plans.

Evaluate past accomplishments—be honest about your feelings about how you are currently spending your time and using your skills. Are you able to check off specific career goals like, going back to nursing school, obtaining a PHD in Marriage & Family Therapy, working a part-time job to learn more about movie production or interning at a publishing company to get experience writing and editing books, etc.

Each year, you should be able to check off accomplishments that were on your envisioned list and recorded goals. By doing so, you are in line with your divine path and following the signs and guidance for your journey, to live your best life.

By making career planning an annual event, you will feel more secure in your career choice and direction – and be better prepared for the many uncertainties and difficulties that lie ahead in all your jobs and careers.

2. Map Your Career Path – One of your first activities when you take on career planning is spending time mapping out your job and career path since the last time you did career planning. If this is the first time, no problem, start from square one, this will be exciting. While you should not dwell on your past, taking time to review and reflect on your previous path, whether straight and narrow, curvy or filled with a

lot of "dead-ends," this process will allow you to plan strategically to become more successful for the future.

Once you've mapped your past, jotted down all your previous jobs, whether you liked them and why, where you are now, and what it takes to get to your next career goal, take time to reflect on your course so far. Has it worked for you? Are you happy with your path? Could you have done things differently? If so, what might you have done differently and why? What specific skills, training or experiences do you need to get where you want to go in your career? You must note them in goal format so you can take action steps to complete them. This will keep you driving in the right direction on your career path.

Here is an example of writing a mapped vision goal, "I will obtain a Master's Degree in Psychology within two years in order to become a licensed Family Therapist and open my own practice within in three years. This year, to get work experience, I'll intern at the neighborhood Outpatient Center"

3. Reflect on Your Needs and Wants, Likes and Dislikes – Change is natural part of life; everybody changes, as do our likes and dislikes. Things we loved doing three years ago may now give us displeasure. In order to evaluate, make a two-column list of your major likes and dislikes as it relates to the workplace. If you like to work with people, travel, and take pictures, but your current job requires that you type memos inside a cubicle all day without social interaction, then this directly conflicts with your true desires. This is an indicator you may want to find opportunities that better align with your career goals.

   As stated earlier, you always want to examine your intentions, take time to really think about what it is you want or need from your work or career. Do you need a corporate environment structure, a creative workspace or more free time with your family during the day? Perhaps you need financial independence. Take time to understand the motives that drive your sense of desire for success and happiness.

4. Examine Your Pastimes and Hobbies –
   Do you think you can't turn a hobby into
   a career? People do it all the time. Career
   planning provides a great time to examine
   the activities you like doing when you're
   not working. Most of the time, the things
   you do when you are not working are
   stress relievers and bring you joy at some
   level. It may sound a bit odd to examine
   non-work activities when doing career
   planning, but it's not. Many times your
   hobbies and leisurely pursuits can give
   great insight into your true desires and
   natural gifts. It provides possible ways to
   incorporate the two in your career paths,
   which will ultimately increase your health
   and wellbeing, and enable you to function
   at a high level professionally.
5. Identify & Use Transferable Skills –
   Some workers are so wrapped up in their
   job titles, they don't see any other career
   possibilities for themselves. Every job
   requires certain skill sets and it is much
   better to categorize yourself in terms of
   these skill sets than be so myopic as to
   focus just on job titles. For instance, I was

coaching a job seeker who was trying to conduct some career planning, but found herself stuck because she identified herself as a Reporter. Once I led her to look beyond her job title and note all the skills she used or had learned doing her job, she was able to see she had many skill sets. She had a strong collection of transferable skills such as television set design, writing, editing, researching, investigating, interviewing, multitasking, meeting production deadlines, and creating media press releases. These skills could easily be applied to a wide variety of other jobs and in many different careers. So while assessing your skills, be sure to look beyond your past job titles and list all of the specific skills you used in that position which can easily transfer to many other jobs.

6. Research Career Categories and Current Job Trends – I believe each person is able to make his or her own job and career opportunities. Even if statistics say your career category is vanishing, if you know what your skill sets are and how to market

yourself, you should be able to find a new job at any time. However, having information about career trends is vital to long-term career planning success.

A career path that is expanding today could easily shrink tomorrow or next year. It is important to see where job growth is expected, especially in the career fields that most interest you. Besides knowledge of these trends, other advantages of conducting research in this area is the power it gives you to adjust and strengthen your professional skills, to stay current, and understand your unique selling points in whatever market you are aiming for.

Keys to job and career success are having a unique set of accomplishments, understanding what your core and transferable skills are, and always seeking to learn more through educational training, on the job experiences, or volunteering to diversify your knowledge base and gain new skills.

Set new goals. Develop a roadmap for your career success by developing specific goals each year. Can you be successful in your career without setting goals? Of course, but you can be much more successful by goal setting.

A major component of career planning is setting short-term (in the coming year) and long-term (beyond a year) career and job goals. Once you initiate this process, another component of career planning is reviewing and adjusting those goals as you achieve career goals or your desires change based on your experiences.

Explore new educational and training opportunities. It sounds a little cliché, but information really is power. Never pass up a chance to learn and grow more as a person, employee, or business owner. A large part of career planning is going beyond passive acceptance of training opportunities to finding new ones that will directly help enhance or further your career.

Take the time to contemplate what types of educational experiences will help you move forward with your personal plan. Look within the company you currently work with, professional associations, local universities and community colleges, as well as online distance learning programs, to find potential career-enhancing opportunities and then find a way participate.

Research opportunities. Career planning is fun because you get to picture yourself in the future. Where will you be in a year? Five years? Ten years? A key component to becoming successful is developing multiple scenarios for yourself, by researching new career paths.

Of course, if you're in what you consider a dead-end job, this activity becomes even more essential for you. All job seekers should take the time to research various career paths, and then develop scenarios for seeing one or more of these visions becoming a reality. Look within your current job situation and career field, but again, as with all aspects of career planning, do not be afraid to look beyond to other possible careers you may never have considered.

Don't Wait, Take Action! Don't wait too long between career planning sessions. Once you begin regularly reviewing and planning your career using the tips provided in this book, you'll find yourself better prepared for whatever lies ahead in your career and in your life. You'll also be more confident in planning for your future by creating the career opportunities you desire through the art of visioning, planning and risk taking. Through faith taking actions towards your true passions.

Pursue your passion…not a paycheck!

Create a Vision Board

Now, we are going to take our planning a step further by creating vision boards and vision maps. You may have heard successful television personalities like Oprah Winfrey talk about the importance of creating vision boards in achieving one's life goals. There are people who seem to respond better to pictures more so than words. Let's get started:

Step 1: Get a piece of paper and write down what you want. Hand write specific goals you envision for your career, love life, marriage, school, health and wealth – all aspects of your life. If you are not sure yet, then write down all of the things you believe will make you happy. For example, you can write about dream vacations, meeting great people, eating delicious food, etc. The sky's the limit, and your personal power lies in your belief and emotional connection to what you want.

Step 2: Prepare all the materials you need to make your Vision Board/s. Get scissors, magazines, photos, and glue, a cork/card board or whatever else you want to use as a surface to attach your pictures. Remember, you can use the internet to find pictures to print and use.

Step 3: Paste/pin all the pictures, sayings, quotes, or whatever you have to your board. Put them in order of importance, or however you see fit to display them. For example, at the center you might place a photo of yourself smiling with a hand full of money, or laying on a beach relaxing with your honey. Remember you are not just putting up pictures; you are imprinting mental images in your brain that will change your emotional state! By looking at you vision board; you want to FEEL the experiences your pictures are portraying.

Step 4: Place your board/s in places you will see daily. Give yourself at least five to ten minutes every day to look at your board and connect with your feeling of gratitude. Imagine you have already acquired everything on your board. Close your eyes and visualize yourself clearly as the happy, grateful person you want to be.

Many psychologist, thought leaders and master teachers suggest the fastest way to acquire the things on your vision board(s) is to visualize, be grateful, be happy and take advantage of the opportunities you have every day. In the process, you will begin to notice the people, events and things you want are finding you instead of you searching so hard for them.

There are many types of vision boards. Below are a few to help you create your best life:

GOAL BOARDS – You should make a goal board if you know exactly what you want to happen in your life. This board serves as a guide to keep you on track on your journey towards achieving your dreams.

THEME BOARDS – Theme boards are helpful when you want specific things to happen by a specific date or in a specific period for a specific occasion. For instance, if you want a new boyfriend before your birthday or Valentine's Day, you will attach photos that reflect that and list dates accordingly.

INSPIRATIONAL BOARDS – Of course, inspirational boards provide inspiration. You would use this type of vision if you are not yet sure of what it is you really want in the future, you just know you want to be happy and feel good about life. On this type of board, it is a good idea to attach pictures of your family, good friends, happy memories, cherished memorabilia, or even snippets of certain inspirational stories or quotes. You can also include your favorite affirmations or sayings from successful and happy people you know.

You may ask yourself, "How many vision boards do I need?" Honestly, you cannot have too many vision boards. Having more than one vision board, or different forms of vision boards, allows you to see your goals almost anywhere you are which keeps your visions alive and on your mind. Place them in your bedroom, office, kitchen, living room or anywhere you constantly see them.

Extend this concept by taking a picture of a board and use that as a screen saver on your computer, tablet or cell phone. No matter how busy you are, you will be able to look at your board and remind yourself of your goals, plans, and the things that make you feel good.

Vision Mapping

Vision mapping is an extension of creating a vision board. It goes a step further outlining a very specific course of action to achieving ones' goals. The process of vision mapping is by far, the most effective strategy to becoming successful in any area of life planning.

Step one is to write the vision clearly. Make it as descriptive as possible. You can describe what you are wearing, the time of day, who you are with, etc. This is when you need to become a kid again and use your imagination.

Step two is goal setting. In this step, make a list of the goals you need to meet in order to achieve that specific area of your dream.

Step three is turning goals into steps. Take the goals you have set and break them down into the steps needed to achieve the goals.

Step four is to turn the steps into tasks. Separate the steps into daily tasks you can complete within your routine.

Step five is to schedule it. You must hold yourself accountable for accomplishing the things you have set out to do within a certain time frame. In order to do so, you need deadlines or completion dates for each step and task.

Turning your dreams into realities doesn't have to be difficult. It requires faith and belief in yourself, a desire to achieve your goals, a vision of the future and action steps to make it happen.

You only get one life. So your choices matter. Pursue what brings you happiness and joy. Money comes and goes, but happiness, peace, joy and fulfillment are priceless.

Whatever the present moment contains, accept it as if you had chosen it.

Eckhart Tolle

KNOW THYSELF, A MAJOR PATH TO SUCCESS

It is essential to know who you are, what you possess internally in terms of gifts/natural talents and externally, in terms of skill sets, education, resources and life experiences that will aid you in getting to the next destination on your journey.

A major part of becoming successful in general, is thoroughly knowing who you are; how you think, your views on life and how you relate to other people. It is important to know your habits, tendencies, how you respond to conflict, fear or challenges and what makes you tick.

There are reasons people do what they do. Everyone is wired a certain way with likes, dislikes and unique personalities. Although it is often difficult for us to understand why we think, act, and feel the way we do, many of the answers for human behavior can be found in what is called human temperaments or personality types.

The study of the human personality goes all the way back to the Greek physician *Hippocrates,* who lived around 460 – 370 BC and is referred to as the "father of medicine". He was born during the prophetic ministries of Nehemiah and Malachi, about 450 years before the birth of Christ. Many have studied his work extensively and still use his personality diagnostic tools in both psychology and psychiatry today.

A generic explanation of human "Temperaments" or "Personalities" is that all of us are born with genetically inherited "behavioral tendencies" that are as much a part of our DNA as is the color of our hair. We are all made up of DNA combinations passed on to us through our parents and ancestors. With this important information being considered, we are better able to understand our basic behavioral dispositions. Behavioral disposition is how a human being acts or conducts him or herself under normal or specified circumstances.

Although a lot of our human personality is inherited, it should also be noted, much of it is influenced and shaped by our unique environments. Most scientific research on human behavior suggests that about 50% of variations in human personality are determined by genetic factors, so our behavior is equally shaped by our environment and by our DNA. All of us have been hard-wired by God, our Creator (Psalm 119:73; 139:13-16; Isaiah 44:24), and we have all been impacted by the world in which we live.

According to scientific analysis, human personalities are commonly divided into four major categories (with the exception of those with severe mental disorders). These four types are further broken down into two categories — *Extroverts* and *Introverts*:

Extroverted Personalities: The *Choleric* and *Sanguine* personality types are more "out-going", sociable, and comfortable in a crowd, even to the extent of standing out in a crowd.

Introverted Personalities: The *Melancholy* and *Phlegmatic* personality types are more shy and "reserved". They feel anxious about being in crowd, especially at the prospect of being singled-out in a crowd.

Generally speaking, all human beings have a degree of each of these four personality types within them. No individual possesses just one personality type, and most have a very strong secondary temperament. I have, provided a sample Personality Test in the back of this book for you to discover which are your dominant characteristics and personality traits, or temperaments.

Each of the four personality types has general strengths and weaknesses with which people must contend, and no one-personality type is better than any other. All four have both good and bad qualities, and all four are necessary to make this world a better place. Whatever your temperament or personality type, God is the one who created you the way you are. He has given you certain abilities and sensitivities for a purpose. That you might faithfully work at developing them and using them in His service. This is often accomplished in your work.

No two people are alike, we are all unique and we have all been given a unique calling, or assignment, in life. Therefore, it is important we not covet qualities we do not possess; rather, we should focus on discovering God's will for our lives, often given to us through Divine revelation, enlightenment, or inspiration in visions and dreams.

The Four Basic Human Temperaments

SANGUINE — The Sanguine temperament is fundamentally impulsive and pleasure seeking. These are your "talkers". They are expressive in personality, desire influence, and are usually social people. The Sanguine is charismatic, generally warm-hearted, pleasant, lively, optimistic, creative, compassionate, and outgoing. In the work environment, he or she is a great volunteer, thrives on compliments, and doesn't hold grudges, but also may struggle with completing tasks, being on time, or remembering obligations. Their decisions are usually based primarily on their feelings. Their workspaces are often frenzied and disorganized. Since they can be a bit impulsive, they often find it difficult to control cravings and are more susceptible to addictive behaviors like smoking, alcohol, or drugs. They are also most susceptible to chemical imbalances and mood disorders. These people feel bored if they are not absorbed by something intriguing and adventurous. The Sanguine is very poor at tolerating boredom, so they will try to avoid monotony and that which is routine at all costs; routine jobs and boring companions annoy and irritate him or her.

Below are a few more traits that describe The Sanguine

- Is self-composed, seldom shows signs of embarrassment; perhaps forward or bold.
- Is eager to express himself before others; likes to be heard.
- Prefers group activities; work or play; not easily satisfied with individual projects.
- Is not insistent upon acceptance of his ideas or plans; compliant and yielding.

- Is good in details; prefers activities requiring pep and energy.
- Is impetuous and impulsive.
- Is keenly alive to their environment, physical and social; curious.
- Tends to take success for granted; is a follower; lacks initiative.
- Is hearty and cordial, even to strangers; forms acquaintanceship easily.
- Not given to worry and anxiety; is carefree.
- Seeks wide and broad range of friendships; is not selective.
- Turns from one activity to another in rapid succession; little perseverance.
- Makes adjustments easily; welcomes changes; makes the best appearance possible.
- Is frank, talkative, sociable, expresses emotions readily; does not stand on ceremony.
- Has frequent fluctuations of mood; tends to frequent alterations of elation and depression.

CHOLERIC — The Choleric temperament is fundamentally ambitious and leader-like. The

Choleric is the strongest of the extroverted temperaments, and is sometimes referred to as a "Type A" personality, "the doer," or "the driver". He or she is a hard driving individual known for accomplishing goals. These folks may have a lot of aggression, energy, and/or passion, which they try to instill in others. Cholerics desire control, and are best at jobs that demand strong control and authority, and require quick decisions and instant attention. The Choleric is the most insensitive of the temperaments; they seem to care little for the feelings of others; feelings simply don't play much into the equation for them. Most Cholerics are men, born leaders who exude confidence. They are naturally gifted businesspeople, strong willed, independent and self-sufficient, they see the whole picture, organize well, insist on production, stimulate activity, thrive on opposition, are unemotional and not easily discouraged. They are decisive, must correct wrongs when they see them, and compulsively need to change things.

In the workplace, they usually systematize everything, are all about independence and do not do well in a subordinate position. They are goal oriented and have a wonderful focus with tasks; usually good at math and engineering, they are analytical, logical and pragmatic; and are masters at figuring things out.

On the other side, they are skeptical and do not trust easily; they need to investigate the facts on their own, relying on their own logic and reasoning. If they are absorbed in something, do not even bother trying to get their attention. Sometimes, they can come across as bossy, domineering, impatient, quick tempered, easily angered, unsympathetic, or domineering.

The Choleric:

- Is self-composed; seldom shows embarrassment, is forward or bold.
- Is eager to express himself before others.
- Is insistent upon the acceptance of his ideas or plans, argumentative and persuasive.
- Is impetuous and impulsive.
- Is self-confident and self-reliant.
- Is very sensitive and easily hurt; reacts strongly to praise or blame.
- Is not given to worry or anxiety.
- Has marked tendency to persevere; does not abandon something readily regardless of success.
- Makes best appearance possible.

PHLEGMATIC — The Phlegmatic temperament is fundamentally relaxed and quiet, then ranges from warmly attentive to lazily sluggish. The Phlegmatic is referred to as the observer or "watcher", they are best in positions of unity and mediation, and solid in positions that desire steadiness.

The Phlegmatic is usually a female who is easygoing, content with herself, calm, cool and collected, tolerant of others, well-balanced, sympathetic, kind, unassuming, keeps emotions hidden, is happily reconciled to life, not in a hurry, has lots of friends, avoids conflict, witty, agreeable and intuitive. Although they are generally very peaceful, patient and adaptable, they tend to be reluctant, indecisive and worriers. They are wonderful at gathering facts, classifying them, and seeing the relationship between them. Basically, they are great at generalizing, seeing the bigger picture, and reading between the lines. They prefer stability to uncertainty and change. Because they are a bit fearful, indecisive and hesitant in life, they have a compromising nature. Socially, they want to know other people's deepest feelings and strive to build intimate attachments with just about everyone in their lives. They are interested in cooperation and interpersonal harmony, this is why they preserve family ties and friendships.

Phlegmatic men and women strive for greater self-knowledge, and seek to contribute to society at large. On the negative side, they are often selfish, self-righteous, judge others easily, resist change, stay uninvolved, dampen enthusiasm, and can be passive-aggressive.

The Phlegmatic:
- Is deliberate; slow in making decisions; perhaps overcautious in minor matters.
- Is indifferent to external affairs.
- Is reserved and distant.
- Is slow in movement.
- Has a marked tendency to persevere.
- Exhibits a constancy of mood.

MELANCHOLIC — The Melancholic temperament is fundamentally introverted and thoughtful. Melancholics are often referred to as "The Thinker". Their analytical personalities desire caution and restraint, best at attending to details and in analyzing problems too difficult for others. They tend to be deep-thinkers and feelers who often see the negative attributes of life, rather than the good and positive things. They are self-reliant and independent and get wholly involved in whatever they are doing.

Melancholies can be highly creative people in activities such as art, literature, music, health-care and ministry, and can become preoccupied with the tragedy and cruelty in the world; they really long to make a significant and lasting difference in the world. Melancholics usually have a high degree of perfectionist tendencies, especially in regards to their own performance. They are usually serious, purposeful, analytical, musical, artistic, talented, creative, self-sacrificing, idealistic, philosophical, and are genius prone. They can be very "introspective" and hold themselves to a very high standard, one that can rarely be achieved.

In the workplace, they tend to be highly organized, schedule oriented, economical, tidy, neat, detail conscious, finish what they start, like charts, graphs, figures and lists, see the problems and are able to identify creative solutions with ease. Sadly, many Melancholics are also victims of deep bouts of depression that comes from dissatisfaction, disappointment, hurtful words or events they have experienced.

Melancholic personalities are people who have a deep love for others, while usually holding themselves in contempt. In short, melancholics take life very seriously and it often leaves them feeling blue, helpless or even hopeless. These folks are extremely caring and are usually our doctors, nurses, social workers, ministers, and teachers.

The Melancholic:

- Is self-conscious, easily embarrassed, timid, and bashful.
- Avoids talking before a group; when obliged to he finds it difficult.
- Prefers to work and play alone. Good with details; careful.
- Is deliberative; slow in making decisions; perhaps overcautious even in minor matters.
- Is lacking in self-confidence and initiative; compliant and yielding.
- Tends to detach socially; is reserved and distant except with intimate friends.
- Tends to suffer from depression; frequently moody or gloomy; very sensitive; easily hurt.
- Worries over possible misfortune; crosses bridges before coming to them.
- Is secretive; not inclined to speak unless spoken to.

- Often represents himself at a disadvantage; modest and unassuming.

Know Your A, B, C and D's

Most people are a unique combination of the four personality types, which are categorized by the letters A, B, C and D. Knowing your personality type as well as that of those with whom you may work, partner with on a business venture or employ is essential to having successful relationships. You will be better equipped to connect with people in a manner that is meaningful to them and more likely not to offend others based on your knowledge of their unique human needs.

As a business owner, understanding the four personality types gives you an advantage when selecting team members, business partners, staff or volunteers and designating job assignments. Ultimately, this information will help you manage business relationships and maintain a healthy work environment. Creating a healthy work environment is key to getting things done more efficiently and being productive; which in my businesses, I equate to being successful.

The "A" personality likes to be in charge and in control of their environment and their lives. They are normally not very detail oriented, choosing to delegate details to others. They are usually very goal oriented and practical in their solutions. However, arriving at their solutions and goals will entail a no-nonsense, "bottom-line" approach.

"A" personalities don't like many restrictions placed on them, prefer to work independently, and desire to set their own schedules. Sometimes, they are workaholics, as they generally put in whatever time and effort is necessary to accomplish their goal.

"A" personality types are usually natural leaders and great in a supervisory or management position. They also tend to have an entrepreneurial streak and may be a business owner or strive to become one someday.

If their job is "routine" or repetitive day by day, they will get bored easily and not enjoy the work. The "A" personality will do whatever is necessary to keep from falling into a pattern or routine; seeking freedom and independence instead. They will also be very dissatisfied if they believe someone is trying to take advantage of them or hold them back.

The "A" personality may not be very good at recognizing their co-worker's feelings and needs, not because they don't care, but because they are so focused on achieving their goals. If you're looking for someone who works well under pressure and seems to excel in high stress situations, the "A" personality is ideal.

The "B" personality is a very energetic, outgoing, and fast paced individual who is generally social. They like to be around people and enjoy being the center of attention. They are good relationship builders and most people gravitate to them right away. With a driving need for approval, they try to please others in hopes that people will like them. Compliments, acknowledgement of their achievements, words of admiration and even applause from groups will be the most important thing you can do for them.

Their biggest fear is being humiliated in public, since it might make people disapprove of them. The "B" personality doesn't want to appear unattractive or unsuccessful, so they will make sure their appearance is impeccable and will always give the impression of being very successful at whatever they are involved in.

Some strengths you can count on from the "B" personality are enthusiasm, outgoing behavior, friendliness towards others and the ability to persuade even the most skeptical of people. They tend to be "dreamers" and can often turn those dreams into very practical ideas in the workplace. "B" personalities are normally spontaneous and use their quick wit and humor to make people like them. They aren't too good about hiding their own feelings either, so if they are hurt or disappointed, it will most likely be very obvious in their mannerisms and overall disposition.

Some of the natural weaknesses associated with the "B" personality type include the tendency to be impatient, a relatively short attention span, and not being very detail oriented. At work, you may find the "B" personalities tend to socialize and spend less time doing their work because they need a lot of social interaction.

The "C" personality is usually a very detail oriented individual that likes to be involved in things that are controlled and stable. They have a need for consistency. They are interested in accuracy, rationality, and logic. People who can't seem to control their emotions may bother them because they believe being emotional makes objectivity difficult or perhaps impossible. Other people's emotions may not be a priority for them, as they tend to strive for the facts and "let the chips fall where they may".

"C" personalities tend to be quite controlling, of both themselves and others. They are very outcome driven and will be sticklers for following procedures and protocol in getting the job done. They are careful, resourceful and above all, are excellent thinkers who will look at all aspects of an issue before taking a stand. Once they take a stand on an issue, they will have the facts to back it up, to be prepared for anyone who challenges them.

They need order; they like their jobs clearly defined and want to know exactly what is expected of them. Knowing the facts, they will be able to prioritize their tasks and see them through to completion.

When in decision making roles, they are cautious, logical and require many details and facts before they make a decision. People who try to sell them something by trying to get them emotionally involved usually fail, because the "C" personality will consider them a "hype artist" and wonder what facts they are trying to hide with all that hype.

In more public roles, the "C" personality will strive for originality, cleverness and uniqueness in whatever they happen to be doing. Many accountants and lawyers are "C" personalities. They are excellent for any job that requires creative thinking based on patience, facts and accuracy.

The "D" personality generally takes a more relaxed approach toward their jobs and life in general. They seek security and longevity on the job and are very happy doing a repetitive task, day in and day out as the repetition allows them to become very skilled in their craft.

An ever-changing or loosely organized work environment may cause them anxiety. Change in general may be an issue for them. Some extreme examples of this would be the bookkeepers who refuse to computerize because they can count on the old way and don't want to change. The "D" will resist change out of concern that even though the current way may be unpleasant, the unknown may be even more unpleasant.

"D" Personality types seek the respect, sincere admiration and acceptance of others and will work hard to please the people they work for as long as they feel appreciated and receive plenty of reassurance they are needed. This satisfies their need for a sense of security.

"D" personalities are usually very organized and being around a messy environment or disorganization will tend to bother them. They are also good at playing a supportive role with others and are normally very caring, thoughtful and compassionate. They are patient, good listeners and will persevere when all others have given up. They especially like working in a group or on a team. They are usually the stabilizing force within that group or team.

Although they may not be as fast as others, they are accurate and thorough. They will usually keep their feelings to themselves and are reluctant to express themselves, even if a more assertive type seems to be taking advantage of them. They will probably choose to "go along to get along" which helps to keep peace at times.

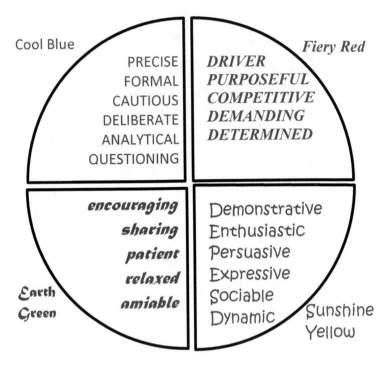

The concept of Personality Colors is based on color psychology. Color psychology suggests that we are able to learn our personality traits by our instinctive color preferences. Whether finding ourselves in conflict with co-workers, family members, neighbors, or the grocery store clerk, the fact remains that we all have a unique personality with its many ways of reacting and interacting.

So, how do we prepare ourselves to interact with those who have a different view of the world?

It's all about discovering our true color. I suggest you do some additional reading into "color psychology". Further study could provide you with additional insight on various theories, which use color energies as a determinant of human behavior. By learning more about this theory, since color is a part of everything, you can better manage yourself and others, as well as gain feelings of control in every situation. You can learn the capacity in which you work best, which will then enhance your career and personal life. Psychic energy cannot be seen. Whether quiet, cautious, gregarious, or bold, there are ways in which we can all better communicate by understanding other energies.

COLORS AND LEADERSHIP STYLE
1. Fiery red
2. Sunshine yellow
3. Earth green
4. Cool blue

Fiery red energy represents the strategic, results-based leaders. A fiery red might live by the motto: *"Only she who attempts the absurd achieves the impossible."*

General attributes of the results-based leader are:
- Positive

- Affirmative
- Bold
- Assertive
- Goal-Directed

Sunshine yellow energy is seen in vision-based leaders. Oprah Winfrey is a sunshine yellow leader. She has crossed racial barriers to succeed in television, publishing, film, education, health & fitness and social awareness. She uses her personal passion to blend public and private; through her own willingness to put everything on the table she inspires people to improve their own lives.

Vision-based leaders are able to communicate with passion, create an inspiring atmosphere, share a vision that other people can believe in, and encourage active participation. General attributes of the vision-based leader are:

- Cheerful
- Uplifting
- Dynamic
- Enthusiastic
- Persuasive

Earth green energy are the People and Values Based Leaders. Mother Teresa is a people and values based (earth green) leader. Her life started without fanfare, a daughter of an Albanian grocer and his wife, she joined a community of Irish nuns and worked as a teacher and high school principal. Then at age 37, she received a call to "serve the poorest of the poor". For the next 50 years, she was the head of Missionaries of Charity - which at the end of her life operated some 517 missions in more than 100 countries. Accepting the Nobel Prize in the name of the "unwanted, unloved and uncared for", she was applauded as a leader known for her values-based and thoughtful planning, her ability to inspire trust and build confidence in others and her model high standards of openness, integrity and respect. General attributes of the value-based leader are:

- Encouraging
- Patient/Calming
- Amiable
- Caring

Cool blue energy representing the information-based leader finishes the color palette. Julie Payette, currently the Chief Astronaut for the Canadian Space Agency, is an example of cool blue energy. Before being recognized for her role with the 1999 Space Shuttle Discovery program, Payette conducted research in computer systems, natural language processing, automatic speech recognition and application of interactive technology in space.

She holds a multi-engine commercial pilot's license, speaks five languages, plays the piano and has sang with various orchestras worldwide. The blue energy leader's strength is in her ability to create structure, process and give detailed analysis, apply critical thinking and make sense of complex details. General attributes of the information-based leader are:

- Precise
- Questioning
- Analytical
- Objective
- Unbiased

Circle your leadership style characteristics:

- Confident and forthright
- Outgoing and optimistic
- Enthusiastic and free-spirited
- Generous, warm and caring
- A non-judgmental mediator and patient
- Loyal and organized
- Detail oriented and reflective

Which of the four primary leadership styles do you fall in?

1. Strategic results-based leaders
2. Vision-based leaders
3. People-based leaders

4. Information-based leaders

By tapping into our own color energy and knowing our personality traits and leadership styles, we become people that are more effective in business. As we open ourselves up to more confidently and wisely communicate with others, we can become more effective in our all domains, whether that domain is home, office, leisure, or anywhere in between.

In order to be successful in anything, you must first KNOW THYSELF

THE INTERNAL SUCCESS
TRANSPORATION SYSTEM

Spiritual gifts is a topic I love to talk about because I really feel once we identify and begin to utilize our spiritual gifts, we will realize they are actually the vehicles that transport us to "destination success" in whatever field we choose.

God has given each of us unique abilities to accomplish specific assignments in our lifetime. By paying attention to our dreams, visions, and areas of passion, we find out more about our potential assignments and what we are placed here to do. By applying our spiritual gifts, our God-empowered abilities to seeing those visions and dreams through, or in selecting career or ministry assignments, we will always operate in a supernatural vein.

Although the topic of spiritual gifts is often used exclusively within the church community or in terms of ministry administration, these same gifts are accessible to every person who believes for all good works, including our career paths. We spend most of our time in the workplace and it is of paramount importance to understand how we can be most efficient and effective with minimal effort; understanding our spiritual gifts will be helpful to do this.

Take a look at the following areas of spiritual gifts and circle the areas you feel best match your specific skill sets or natural abilities:

Administration (the gift of serving) – The special ability God gives to steer people towards the accomplishment of goals and directives by planning, organizing, and supervising others.

The divine enablement to understand what makes an organization function and the special ability to plan and execute procedures that accomplish the goals of a ministry, business or organization.

People with this gift:

- Develop strategies or plans to reach identified goals.
- Assist groups to become more effective and efficient.
- Create order out of organizational chaos.
- Manage or coordinate a variety of responsibilities to accomplish a task.
- Organize people, tasks, or events.

Apostle/Leader/Business   Planter – (Leadership Gift) – This special ability assists in exercising general leadership or oversight over a number of churches, businesses, or civic organizations with an authority in spiritual advisory matters, which is readily recognized. In the strictest sense, it is the gift whereby the Spirit appoints certain Christians to lead, inspire and develop the churches of God by the proclamation and teaching of biblical doctrine. An extension of the utilization of this gift in the market place would be developing and overseeing multiple community outreach organizations that may not be traditional churches, but are founded on biblical doctrine, training leaders in spiritual matters, and providing outreach or evangelistic programs to help people in need.

People with this gift:

- Pioneer and establish new ministries, churches, or spiritually focused charitable organizations.
- Adapt to different surroundings by being culturally sensitive and aware.
- Desire to counsel or help the unreached people in the community or in other countries.
- Demonstrate authority and long-term vision for the development of global missions and ministry work.

Celibacy - The special ability God gives to some to voluntarily remain single without regret and with the ability to maintain control over sexual impulses to serve God without distraction. People with this gift have dedicated their lives totally to the work of ministry as God gives them instruction on a daily basis.

People with this gift:

- Remain single to be able to devote themselves completely to their relationship with God or ministry, i.e. monks and nuns.
- Have other gifts they are able to use more effectively in the world as God instructs, because they are celibate.

Craftsman / Artist – This gift allows a person to create artistic expressions that produce a spiritual response of strength and inspiration. This gift enables someone to create, build, maintain, or repair things.

People with this gift:

- Work with wood, cloth, paint, metal, glass, and other raw materials.

- Make things that increase the effectiveness of other people's lives.
- Design and build tangible items and resources for houses, businesses, or ministry use.
- Work with different kinds of tools and are skilled with their hands.
- Develop and use artistic skills such as drama, writing, art, music, dance, etc.
- Challenge people's perspective of God and their beliefs through various forms of the arts.

Discernment / Distinguishing Spirits – The special ability God gives to some, which allows them to know "the motive behind an action"; they are able to sense with assurance whether certain behavior or teaching is from God, Satan, human error, or human power. This gift is extremely important in all areas of our lives, specifically business because with it, one is able to "see in advance" whether they should proceed or not in relationships with others. It helps to guide decision-making as one has foreknowledge in situations. So while things that would have blind-sided another person, the discerner, is prepared, able to adapt and govern themselves appropriately.

People with this gift:

- Distinguish truth from error, right from wrong, pure motives from impure when interacting with others.
- Identify deception in others with accuracy and appropriateness.
- Recognize inconsistencies in a spiritual teaching, prophetic message, or interpretation of a God-given message.
- Are able to sense the presence of evil.

Encouragement (Speaking Gift) – The special ability to offer comfort, words of encouragement, hope, and reassurance to discouraged, weak, or troubled people so they are consoled. The people with this gift uplift your spirit and generally make you feel better after having been in their presence.

People with this gift:

- Come to the side of those who are discouraged to reassure them and give them hope.

- Inspire others; they emphasize God's promises and give others confidence to move forward in life despite adversity.

Evangelism / Evangelist – The special ability to proclaim the Gospel of salvation effectively so people respond and wish to enter into relationship with God.

People with this gift:

- Communicate the message of Christ with clarity and conviction.
- Seek out opportunities to talk to unbelievers about spiritual matters.
- Challenge unbelievers to faith and to become fully devoted followers of Christ.
- Adapt their presentation or conversation about God and the Gospel to be able to connect with the unique and individual's needs of all kinds of people.
- Seek opportunities to build relationships with unbelievers and God in and outside of church especially by way of their businesses.

Exhortation (Speaking Gift) – The special ability to help strengthen the weak, faltering and fainthearted in such a way that they are motivated to be all God wants them to be in every area of their lives. These people push others to reach their full potential by way of encouraging, challenging, comforting, and guiding. This gift is the divine enablement to present truth to urge one to action, especially those who are discouraged or wavering in their faith.

People with this gift:
- Come to the side of those who are weak in spirit to strengthen them.
- Challenge or confront others to trust and hope in the promises of God.
- Urge others to action by applying Biblical truth.
- Offer others advice, provide an outline for solutions, or a strategy for making progress in life so they may become their best self.

Faith - The special conviction God gives to some to be firmly persuaded of God's power and promises to accomplish His will and purpose and to display such a confidence in Him and His Word that circumstances and obstacles do not shake that conviction; an unwavering belief in God's ability to fulfill His purposes in all situations of your life.

People with this gift:

- Believe the promises of God and inspire others to do the same.
- Act in complete confidence of God's ability (not their abilities) to do the "impossible", to overcome any presented obstacles that block them from destiny.
- Advance God's will and purposes often because they go forward when others will not. They are innovators, trailblazers and history-makers.
- Simply ask God for what they need and trust Him fully for his provision.

Giving – (Serving Gift) – The gift that enables a believer to recognize God's blessings in their lives and to respond by generously, sacrificially, and cheerfully giving of one's resources (time, talent, and treasure) to others without thought of return.

People with this gift:

- Manage their finances and limit their lifestyle in order to give as much of their resources as possible.
- Support the work of ministry or giving to the needy sacrificially.
- May have a special ability to make money so that they may use it to further good and charitable works.

Healing (Sign Gift) – The special ability God gives to some to serve as a human instrument to cure illness and restore health (physically, emotionally, mentally, or spiritually) apart from the use of natural means. This is a divine enablement to be God's means for restoring people to wholeness.

People with this gift:

- Demonstrate the power of God to bring healing and restoration to the sick, diseased, and oppressed of the world.
- Pray, touch, or speak words that miraculously bring healing to one's body, mind, or soul.

Helps / Serving – (Serving Gift) – The gift that enables a person to work gladly behind the scenes with little to no recognition necessary for them to do their assignment. It is the divine enablement to accomplish practical and necessary tasks, which free-up, support, and meet the needs of others.

People with this gift:

- Serve behind the scenes whenever needed to support the gifts and ministries, business operations of others (without having to be asked).
- See the tangible and practical things to be done and enjoy doing them.
- Sense God's purpose and pleasure in meeting every day responsibilities.
- Attach spiritual value to practical service.
- Enjoy knowing that they are freeing up others to do what God has called them to do.
- Would rather do a job than find someone else to do it.

Hospitality (Serving Gift) – The special ability to provide an open home and warm welcome to those in need of food, lodging, or newcomers coming into an area in general for fellowship.

People with this gift:

- Provide an environment where people feel valued and cared for.
- Create a safe and comfortable setting where relationships can develop.
- Seek ways to connect people together into meaningful relationships.
- Set people at ease in unfamiliar surroundings.

Intercession / Prayer (Serving Gift) – The ability to pray for extended periods of time on a regular basis for others sacrificially.

People with this gift:
- Feel compelled to earnestly pray on behalf of someone or some cause.
- Have a daily awareness of the spiritual battles being waged and pray.
- Are convinced God moves in direct response to prayer.
- Pray in response to the leading of the spirit, whether they understand it or not.
- Exercise authority and power for the protection of others and the

equipping of them to serve or fulfill their life purposes.

Knowledge (Speaking Gift) – The special gift that enables a person to understand in an exceptional way the great truths of God's Word and to make them relevant to specific situations in the world. This gift gives a person insight or revelation on how to apply Biblical principles in life.

People with this gift:
- Receive truth, which enables them to make better decisions.
- Gain supernatural knowledge on how to solve issues.

Visionary/Leadership (Serving Gift) – This ability allows some to set goals in accordance with God's purposes for life and to communicate these goals to others in such a way that they voluntarily and harmoniously work together to accomplish the goals. The divine enablement to cast vision, motivate, and direct people to help bring the vision to fruition.

People with this gift:
- Provide direction for people or ministry or in the marketplace.
- Motivate others to perform to the best of their abilities.

- Present the "big picture" for others to see and help to accomplish.
- Model the values for others; lead by example and take responsibility for their actions by also working towards the vision that they speak of.

Mercy / Compassion (Serving Gift) – This gift enables a person to feel exceptional empathy and compassion for those who are suffering (physically, mentally, or emotionally); they are moved by genuine sympathy for others who are hurting and respond by speaking words of compassion and caring for the needy in love to alleviate their distress.

People with this gift:
- Focus on alleviating the sources of pain or discomfort in suffering people and animals.
- Address the needs of the lonely and forgotten of the world.
- Serve in difficult or unsightly circumstances for the sake of others.

- Concern themselves with individual or social issues that oppress people.

Miracles (Sign Gift) – A person with this gift serves as a human intermediary through whom God performs acts of supernatural power that are recognized by others which alter the ordinary course of nature and authenticate the divine commission to bring people into relationship with God.

People with this gift:

- Speak God's truth and may have it authenticated by an accompanying miracle.
- Declare God to be the source of all miracles and themselves vessels through which He operates for His glory.

Missionary (Leadership Gift) – This gift urges and allows people to minister their specific gifts to people in another culture or foreign countries.

People with this gift:

- Have an intense spirit of unease at the thought of not reaching all of the people in distress or those not in relationship with God across the globe.

- Establish meaningful relationships with people of other nationalities or cultures effortlessly.

Music – This gift gives a person the capability to uplift and inspire others through instruments, music, singing, or dancing.

People with this gift:

- Sing or play a musical instruments quite well, and enjoy it very much.
- See that their singing or instrument playing is encouragement for others.

Pastor / Shepherd – This gift enables some to assume a long-term personal responsibility for the leadership and spiritual care, protection, guidance, and feeding (teaching) of a group of Believers. This gift also enables a person to nurture, care for, and develop people into spiritual maturity.

People with this gift:

- Take responsibility to nurture the whole person (mind, body, and soul) in their walk with God and in life in general.

- Provide spiritual guidance and oversight to a group of people.
- Model discipleship with their life; are devoted followers of God.

Poverty (voluntary) – The special ability God gives to some to purposely live an impoverished lifestyle to serve and aid others with their material resources, to renounce material comfort and luxury and adopt a personal lifestyle equivalent to those living at the poverty level in a given society in order to serve God and others more effectively.

People with this gift:
- Will often choose to live among people who are considered poverty-stricken.
- Live at a poverty level although they have the means to live at a higher standard.
- Choose this lifestyle in order to minister to the poor more effectively through being able to relate and have more compassion.

Prophet / Prophecy (Special Gift) – This gift allows some to proclaim the Word of God with clarity and to apply it fearlessly in any situation with a goal of strengthening, encouraging, and bringing comfort to others. This gift also gives one the ability to receive divine insight and revelation to make better decisions, help others to see the right path to take, or avoid.

People with this gift:
- Expose sin or deception in others for the purpose of bringing one into a closer relationship with God/life purpose.
- Speak a timely word from God causing conviction, repentance, and edification; their words often bring life to dead situations, give supernatural hope and the ability to overcome challenges blocking destiny.

Teaching / Teacher – Has the ability to explain the spiritual truths and principles of life so others may easily understand and apply them and consequently grow and develop into the highest form of themselves.

People with this gift:
- Communicate effectively; they inspire others to reach for and live their best life by learning necessary life lessons along the way.

- Challenge listeners simply and practically to grow.
- Give attention to detail and accuracy; are always expanding their knowledge base by reading and learning themselves.

Tongues (interpreting) – The special ability to speak and/or interpret God-given messages (that are divinely downloaded and spoken in foreign or unknown languages). Speaking in tongues is also referred to as speaking directly to God or in a heavenly language.

Speaking in tongues is an ability given to all who believe to use in prayer or praise; this is a language spoken in faith, it has never been previously learned but when spoken, unbelievers can hear God's message in their own language. If a tongue is spoken without another person being present who has the gift of interpretation of tongues, then it is for the person to connect directly with God and edify himself or herself.

People with this gift:
- Pray for the needs of others in the spiritual realm, making their prayer more effective than speaking in their natural language.

- Spontaneously give messages from God, which is interpreted by another person.
- Speak in a language they have never learned and do not understand.
- Worship the Lord with unknown words that are too deep for the mind to comprehend; it is a spiritual, heavenly language.
- Experience an intimacy with God, which inspires them to serve and edify others more.

Wisdom (Speaking Gift) – This gift allows a person to sort through opinions, facts, and thoughts in order to determine what solution would be best for the individual or others who are seeking assistance or advice. Wisdom is the ability to apply knowledge to life situations in a way that makes spiritual truths very relevant and practical with decision-making and daily life circumstances.

People with this gift:
- Focus on the unseen consequences in determining what the proper next steps are for a person to take.

- Receive a special understanding of what is necessary to meet the needs of others as well as their own.
- Provide Divine insight and solutions to those in the midst of conflict and confusion.

Writing – The gift that gives a person the ability to express truth in a written form; a form that can edify, instruct and strengthen others. This is a special ability to formulate thoughts and ideas into a meaningful written structure. The reader will find courage, guidance, knowledge, or edification through the words he or she reads.

People with this gift:

- Write stories, sermons, devotions, prayers, songs, or poetry and are inspired to uplift, educate, or share a message with people.
- May be better at expressing their thoughts in written form than verbal.

USING YOUR GIFTS TO CHOOSE THE RIGHT CAREER PATH

The things that come naturally to us, the tasks we perform effortlessly, the ones we often take for granted are our spiritual gift. We may think there is nothing special about our innate abilities and assume these things are easy for others as well, but this is not true.

As a business owner and leader within the beauty industry, one of my greatest joys is being able to make contact with so many people in so many capacities. Whether the person I meet is a client, student, mentee, or colleague, I naturally encourage them to recognize their natural gifts. More often than not, when I point out the natural gifts I see in them, they don't think there is anything special about those specific qualities. Their gifts are a part of their personality, and they just see them as "who they are". I am referring to gifts such as great musical, artistic, or athletic ability but also to those unique personality and character traits that actually assist you in accomplishing your work or passion with ease.

Knowing your natural gifts and your personality type can be very helpful in career development. The more closely your work aligns with your personality and natural ability, the more satisfaction and success you will have professionally, it will become more of an effortless process.

Below is a list of nine major personality types with their gifts. Be sure to note the set of qualities that fit most closely with you, you may identify with several. Sometimes the people closest to us can more readily identify our gifts, but circle anything that jumps out at you.

1. High sense of integrity, disciplined, hard-working, conscientious, purposeful, idealistic, well-organized, responsible, good attention to detail.

2. Helpful to others, generous, supportive, warm, empathetic, caring, self-sacrificing, likable.

3. Goal-focused, motivating and inspiring to others, ambitious, competent, confident, adaptable; a role model.

4. Creative, sensitive, intuitive, empathetic, aesthetic sensible, intuitive, introspective, authentic to self.

5. Keen observer, perceptive, knowledgeable, innovative, expert in their field, problem-solver, curious, calm under

pressure, strong-willed, confident, and highly concentrated on targeted tasks.

6. Committed, loyal, team player, trustworthy, well-prepared, responsible, trouble-shooter, keen wit, hardworking, persistent.

7. Enthusiastic, optimistic, high energy, spontaneous, engaging, people-person, quick thinker, versatile, synthesizer of ideas.

8. Self-confident, decisive, risk-taker, protective of others, charismatic, self-reliant, takes initiative, natural leader.

9. Peacekeeper, mediator, compassionate, empathetic, giving.

How could knowing your natural personality characteristics be helpful when evaluating your career fit? As an example, if a person with the #8 qualities is considering a job that would not allow her to take on a leadership role and she has little decision-making power, she is likely to be frustrated, and to a large degree her natural gifts are going to be wasted.

If an individual is most like #6, she will do best in a work environment that is collaborative and supportive, where her hard work and loyalty are not taken for granted, and she is able to look ahead and problem-solve.

Someone with the traits of #9 has a natural gift for conflict resolution and mediation. This knowledge directly gives career guidance and direction as it relates to "best-fit" placements in specific fields or tasks. By getting a great grasp on this information, you will better understand your strengths and weaknesses in the workplace; you'll understand where your lane is and make all efforts to stay in it so you will arrive at your desired destination more quickly.

Knowing Thyself Leads to Success in Business

Does personality matter in becoming a successful entrepreneur? Recent studies say yes. Successful entrepreneurs share a number of common personality traits, and these traits are the predominant indicators of their success outweighing education, family ties, skills and experience.

Moreover, people who choose business ventures that are in sync with their true personalities tend to experience the greatest level of success and fulfillment in general because they are "being themselves", their truest selves.

Every personality type and therefore, every person has the potential to grow a successful business. You just need to determine the right opportunity for you. Self-awareness guides you in understanding what's needed to bridge the gap between who you are and what the opportunity you find requires. This is a major theme of this book, even over finding specific business ventures, which I will address in later chapters. Knowing yourself, your capabilities and tapping into what you do well naturally, all help to lay the foundation for you being the best version of you and thus more successful in whatever you choose to do.

Much research shows that most entrepreneurs who reach their goals are often natural leaders, strong problem-solvers and work well under pressure. For those who don't have this type of personality, which is most of the population, it is critical to understand the requirements for being a successful entrepreneur. Only then will you be prepared to create the right team for the endeavor.

The key to success is your business and team selection: You must select an opportunity that best suits your personality, then hire or select the right people to surround yourself with to meet the skill requirements for that particular venture. No one person has it all; teamwork makes the dream work. Once you have identified your strengths and weaknesses, you should have a good understanding of the skill sets you need to add to your team in the areas you are personally lacking. That is using wisdom.

Research has found that most highly successful entrepreneurs have a few basic general skill sets, gifts, and personality characteristics that assist them in their leadership. Below are those main categories along with a few pointers in selecting team members that would best complement you based on your strengths and weaknesses.

Entrepreneurial Personalities

Trailblazers are very competitive, ambitious and goal oriented; so much so that you tend to be aggressive and sometimes take a steamroller approach. You're restless and energetic, with a strong drive and a sense of urgency, regardless of the task at hand. You tend to have two speeds, fast and faster. Independent, persistent and decisive, you aren't happy unless you're in charge. You are a calculated risk taker. You are logical, analytical, practical and realistic so you tend to base decisions on facts rather than feelings.

The Trailblazer's Business Strengths: Good industries for you could include the medical, technology, finance, legal and consulting fields. Being a strong strategic thinker, you focus easily on marketing and operations. Your challenge is likely to be working with people. You are usually a better leader than manager and need to surround yourself with others who can manage the people side of the business.

Trailblazers prefer being the driving force of a business. You typically wouldn't buy a franchise or distributorship, but you would start a company that competes with a franchise. You're highly innovative, especially when it comes to taking an idea to the next level.

Go-Getters have a higher-than-average level of both dominance and sociability and are very driven and independent. You are competitive, but your drive to succeed is sometimes tempered by your interest in and concern for others. Much research on the traits of successful entrepreneurs shows that Go-Getters represent the largest percentage of business founders. Your natural style lends itself to leading and managing both people and processes.

Go-Getters show a lot of initiative, combined with a compelling sense of urgency to get things done. They are typically good leaders and good managers, usually excelling at motivating themselves and those around them well.

The Go-Getter's Business Strengths: Retail is a great industry for you, but you may prefer being the outside rainmaker. You work well in ambitious and unfamiliar environments. This means you can invest in, buy or start a business that's totally new to you and still make a success of it. You don't need to be an expert in the field to start the business; you are a good collaborator and can learn as you go while brining on the necessary team members to make the business venture work.

Specialists are usually the experts of our world. You are very analytical, relatively risk-averse and anti-selling. Specialists generate most of their new business from referrals and networking. They mainly measure success based on their personal income.

Specialists are tactically oriented, prefer being responsible for areas within their area of expertise, are more detail-oriented, and prefer environments that provide both security and stability. Specialists are typically more risk-averse, unless they are working within their area of expertise.

Generalists are strategic thinkers. They are big picture-oriented people who prefer environments where they can use their results-driven nature, enjoy autonomy and independence, and are stronger risk-takers.

Generalist personalities have a dominance factor that is much greater than their compliance factor. This is the source of their need to win and their belief that they are always right. They are self-confident and able to assume more risk. The Generalist personality has a compliance factor that is much greater than the dominance factor. Therefore, doing things by the book-following rules, policies and procedures is more important to them. They will try to do everything right, which means avoiding risks.

Managers are dominant and independent. In your case, these two characteristics feed each other, so you can appear to be even more dominant or independent than you actually are sometimes. You are also very goal-oriented and can be quite analytical, focusing more on processes and outcomes than on people. In this case, there is a tendency to look at people only as vehicles for helping you accomplish your goals. Consequently, you sometimes disregard or overlook the people part of the equation or unwittingly offend people with your straightforward communication style.

Managers, unlike the previous two entrepreneurial types, have a higher-than-average level of relaxation and know that some projects simply take more time to complete and some goals take longer to achieve than others. You're loyal, at times to a fault, as you consider your employees to be an extension of your family. You can deal well with customers, especially repeat customers, so often; you are great at growing new businesses.

The Manager's Business Strengths: You like doing things on your own, are a great behind-the-scenes leader and love working with systems, concepts, ideas and technologies. You excel at competitive selling because you enjoy overcoming rejection and achieving goals despite obstacles. Managers enjoy working by themselves, and managing others can be a challenge, so hiring employees who are exceptional listeners and engage well with others would be a good idea.

Motivators have a high level of sociability, an above-average level of dominance, and are both independent and driven. This gives you the ability to work well under pressure and in autonomous situations. It also means you will be a great consensus builder, a good collaborator and a driving force of change.

The Motivator's Business Strengths: Retail can be a great fit for you--or any environment where people are a large part of the equation. You do well in almost any business that involves sociability, as long as it's a somewhat non-confrontational environment. You can be convincing and avoid most confrontation by creating a strong emotional argument.

Motivators do well in the toughest of customer service roles, as you are able to see both sides of the argument. Motivators are good at nurturing relationships and often do best in a business that involves keeping clients for the long term and thrive in a team environment.

Authorities are the backbone of our society. They are the loyal workers who make our world function. You make our products, services and systems and always do it right. As an Authority, you may not always be the best founder of an entrepreneurial enterprise, but you can be an excellent distributor, franchisee or owner of an existing business. You often do well when you purchase an ongoing operation.

Authorities are detail- and tactic-oriented and are motivated by doing things one way, the right way. You are very conscientious and cooperative, following rules, procedures and policies carefully. Very thorough with details, you're cautious, deliberate, logical and analytical. At times, you're also relaxed, patient and accommodating by nature, you are great team players who tend to avoid confrontation. Examples of businesses that fit this personality type would be dry cleaning stores and liquor or convenience stores, where the need for the product or service is strong. You grow your customer base, embracing them with loyalty, you see your customers as an extension of your family.

The Authority's Business Strengths: Authorities often refer to themselves as "accidental" entrepreneurs, because they may end up running a business that was never part of their original plan. Consequently, you're best served by going into a business that embraces your level of expertise or allows you to develop a new level of expertise. Since you do have an accommodating nature, you may dislike prospecting, so an ideal business for you is one where customers or clients are driven to you.

Most authorities need a partner with a stronger natural ability to solicit, prospect or network. You can be very successful buying a franchise or business venture, as long as the organization is well supported with advertising and marketing, which is often outside of your natural skill-set.

Collaborators and Authorities are similar but the major difference in the two is that collaborators have a personality gift called sociability. This characteristic allows you to use your influence to get what you want. It's all about people; you relish the people side of business.

You typically benefit from having a partner who is more aggressive about developing new business. Collaborators usually aren't comfortable with cold calling or pitching new ideas; you like to follow prescribed rules and guidelines.

The Collaborator's Business Strengths: You're good at running customer service-oriented or retail businesses, or any business where being convincing is an important aspect of getting the job done, and done right. From an entrepreneurial perspective, Collaborators do well within structured environments where people are an element of success.

Collaborators can be great salespeople in a warm selling market because they use their sociability to sell their expertise. Warm selling means you bring the prospect to you, often through a letter or advertisement enticing the prospect to contact you for more information about your product or service. Once prospects do get in touch, your expertise takes over, and you sell your heart out!

Diplomats are restless and enjoy working under a certain amount of pressure. You get things done quickly and work well with deadlines. You adjust easily to change and deal well with new situations. You have a high sense of urgency and like variety because of your compliance nature and need to do things right, you work at your full capacity. You multitask and keep a variety of things going at once. Active and energetic, you vigorously attack the parts of your business that you enjoy. You can experience difficulty in delegating details, but do a great job when you can do the work yourself.

Diplomats are considered the best of the Specialist entrepreneurs, as they have both sociability and drive in their personalities. These are two important elements to success. You are not the greatest rainmaker, but once you have a client or prospect, you do a great job of keeping them happy.

The Diplomat's Business Strengths: You excel in retail or other people-oriented environments. Both outgoing and empathetic, you tend to be well liked, but you sometimes have a hard time asserting yourself and holding others accountable. Therefore, to successfully lead a company, you typically need to hire stronger, more results-oriented personalities to be sure deadlines are met, commitments are kept and staff members follow through on their duties.

Putting It All Together

There's a great deal of truth to the notion that entrepreneurs are born, not made. Although our upbringings, belief systems, education, training and development affect our ultimate behaviors, our core personalities remain relatively constant throughout our lives.

The most important factors that distinguish entrepreneurs who barely make it from those who make millions are personality and sometimes more important, the ability to harness our personality, use it and learn from it. The most successful entrepreneurs know that the greatest knowledge is self-knowledge. They understand how to make the best of their talents and manage or compensate for their weaknesses or potential limitations.

Each of the entrepreneurial personalities provided are more compatible with some types of businesses than others. It's best to choose a business that is well suited to your natural personality and behavioral style, rather than swim upstream with the currents going against your success. I recommend going with the flow and focusing on pursuing the types of businesses in which you can naturally thrive.

In essence, by understanding your own personality, you can leverage your strengths, work to improve your weaknesses and limitations and discover the type of career or business that will work best for you. You can then choose an opportunity that fits your leadership personality and select team members who excel in the areas in which you may be limited. To do more personal discovery, we have included a personality assessment at this back of this book.

IS THERE AN ENTREPRENEUR IN YOU?

The reason I put so much emphasis on the need to learn who you are, your likes, dislikes, desires, hopes, dreams, personality type, inner gifts, and general skill sets is because, to be successful in business you must first, know thyself. To get along well with others, which is a huge part of business; you must first know thyself and get along with you well.

The real key to doing anything exceptional in life is knowing and being true to yourself, being authentic. I recommend a lot of soul searching before you decide to start a business that employs others, so the proper groundwork, your foundation, is correctly built.

I mentioned that I learned early on that I was an entrepreneur; around age 9 or so, others could tell I possessed certain personality traits they likened to being business leadership characteristics. I believe my upbringing and the things I was exposed to as a young child influenced me as well. Seeing my aunt operate a home daycare business as a young girl exposed me to the idea of "doing your own thing" or being a business owner. Even then, as a young child, I remember figuring out ways to streamline and make my aunt's business more efficient and productive while helping her with odd duties in her daycare. I believe I have entrepreneurial DNA and was born to start my own business. This does not mean that because I was "born to do it" that it is easy.

Later, I had to give honor to my aunt who took a huge step years ago to go against the grain and be her own boss. In my adulthood, after starting my own business, I found that starting a business is a lot of work. Even with the best business concept, team, sense of faith and vision, it's still very challenging. Anyone who tells you it's not is either lying or has never actually started one themselves. The hours are long, the sacrifices are great and you are bombarded with issues, challenges, and problem upon problem with seemingly no end in sight at times. If you don't have the constitution to weather these things, your business could implode on you faster than it started.

Entrepreneurship is not for everyone. You can begin to find out if it's for you by assessing your skills, personality and abilities as the leader because, for the most part, you'll be doing a lot of the upfront work by yourself unless you have the start-up funds to hire a full staff to operate your enterprise. If you can't lead yourself through startup, chances are you won't likely be able to lead your business and future employees through growth and on to success.

Successful entrepreneurs, from Henry Ford to Steve Jobs, share similar qualities. Look at the following qualities to see how many of them you possess:

Leadership - Leaders are born, not made. Do you find yourself being the go-to person for others most of the time? Do you find people asking your opinion or to help guide or make decisions? Have you been in management roles throughout your career?

A leader is someone who values the goal over any unpleasantness the work project may bring. A leader is more than just tenacious, they are strong communicators and have the ability to amass a team of people toward a common goal in a way that the entire team is motivated and works effectively to get there as a team, they are visionaries. They earn the trust and respect of their team by demonstrating positive professional qualities and confidence, then fostering an environment that proliferates these values through team effort. A leader is someone who will also follow when necessary.

Self-Motivated – If you need someone to jump-start you then entrepreneurship is probably not the best professional track for you. Most of the famous entrepreneurs in history are leaders with intense personalities. Nobody makes progress by sitting back and waiting for progress to happen or opportunity to find them. Successful people go out into the world and invoke change through their actions. Typically, they enjoy challenges and will work tirelessly to solve problems when confronted. They are versatile and adapt well to changing situations without unraveling. Self-motivated leaders are typically experts in helping their teams change by motivating them toward new goals and opportunities.

Successful entrepreneurs are driven by a bigger picture, a vision rather than just the task at hand. They are able to think on a more universal level in this regard. They are also often very passionate about their ideas that drive them toward their goals and are notoriously difficult to steer off course once they get started.

Values, Ethics & Integrity – I would venture to say that anyone can start a business, but it takes a certain caliber of person to be able to maintain a successful business. Businesses are sustainable because there is a universally understood code of ethics that underpins the very fabric upon which commerce is conducted. Successful, sustainable business people maintain the highest standards of integrity because, at the end of the day, if you cannot prove yourself a credible businessperson, then no one will do business with you and you are out of business.

Not Afraid of Failure – Successful entrepreneurs are risk takers who have gotten over one very significant hurdle, they are not afraid of failure. That's not to say they rush in with reckless abandon. In fact, entrepreneurs are often successful because they are calculating and able to make the best decisions in even the worst scenarios. However, they also accept that even if they make the best decisions possible, things may not always go according to plan. They know they could possibly fail despite their best efforts. I'm sure you have heard the old adage, "nothing ventured, nothing gained", that's exactly what I'm saying here. To be a successful businessperson, you cannot be afraid to fail, put it out there and give it your best shot. There are no successful entrepreneurs just sitting on their couch asking themselves "what if?" They will try to find out. If they don't succeed the first time, they'll try again and again, and again until they do.

Extreme Innovators – Successful entrepreneurs are often defined by their constant drive to develop new ideas and improve on existing systems and processes. In fact, that's how most of them got into business; they identified an issue with an existing system or process and created a solution. Successful people welcome change and often depend on it to improve their effectiveness as leaders and business owners.

Be honest about what you don't know – While entrepreneurs are typically strong personalities overall, the most successful ones have learned that there's always a lesson to be learned from everything. They are rarely afraid to ask questions when it means the answers will provide them with the insight needed to move a vision forward. Successful entrepreneurs are confident, but not egotistic to the point that their bull-headedness is a weakness that blocks them from seeing the bigger picture and ultimately making the best decisions for their business or product brands.

Play to Win – Entrepreneurs generally enjoy a challenge and like to win. This is necessary since starting a business is one of the biggest challenges a person can take on in their lifetime. In business, it's a constant war and competition in the marketplace. It's also a personal challenge to focus inward and grow a business from nothing into a financial powerhouse.

Strong Support Networks – In almost every case, entrepreneurs never arrive at destination success alone. The best understand that it takes a network of contacts, business partners, financial partners, peers and resources to succeed in this game. Effective business leaders nurture these relationships and surround themselves with people who can help make them become more effective. Any good leader is only as strong as the team that supports them.

GETTING DOWN TO BUSINESS

I'm a firm believer that there are opportunities all around us; if we seek, we shall find. A great way to get your feet wet in different types of business ventures is to take on a non-traditional project online as an independent contractor, part-time employee, or purchase shares in an existing successful venture.

We are blessed with a powerful tool called the internet and it offers all the information you need about any subject. The internet is the leading source of business commerce as well. Now days, mostly everything is done online. With the click of a mouse, far away from traditional office settings, millions of business transactions take place 24-hours a day. As such, there are infinite possibilities when it comes to connecting to or beginning an online venture. Begin to think outside the box of just "office work" as you look for new creative ways to bring in more income; look into "home-based" or "online businesses" as options.

Be careful with online businesses because there are many scammers out there. Spend time researching the website and the company represented. Check out the contact information, see if there is either an email address or a contact icon then send a short message expressing your interest in the internet business and see if you receive a response. Check also to see if there is a physical address on the website as this adds credibility.

You also want to look for logos such as the Better Business Bureau, Truste.org, or i-Corp.org on the business website. Click on these logos and you should see detailed information about the business. You can also look up the domain name on the DomainTools.com (previously called Who is) Website and you will see the registration details on that particular company.

At the end of the day, once you have researched the internet business opportunity thoroughly, contacted the representatives and asked a lot of questions, pray about it, sleep on it and follow what your research is telling you. After all, most things are learned by trial and error and you must take some risks to succeed in anything. I suggest you take calculated risks though and do your homework before you invest any time or money.

Business Opportunity Defined

So, exactly what is a business opportunity? I've used the term broadly but will now get into the technicalities of the topic. I often get many questions about this in business workshops from those who are testing the waters as entrepreneurs and trying to decide whether to buy a current independent business, a franchise, or start a small business. I will attempt to allay the confusion by giving a simple analogy.

Remember in elementary school when your teacher explained the difference between a rectangle and a square? She probably said something like, a square is also a rectangle, but a rectangle isn't necessarily a square. Well, the same relationship exists between business opportunities, independent businesses for sale and franchises. All franchises and independent businesses for sale are business opportunities, but not all business opportunities meet the requirement of being a franchise nor are they in the strictest sense of the word independent businesses for sale.

Before getting involved in any type of business venture, it is ALWAYS important to check the legal guidelines regarding the specifics on it as each state has laws defining business opportunities and regulating their sales. Not all state laws define business opportunities in the same manner. Most of them however, use the following general criteria to define them:

A **business opportunity** involves the sale or lease of any product, service, equipment, etc. that will enable the purchaser-licensee to begin a business.

- The licensor or seller of a business opportunity declares that it will secure or assist the buyer in finding a suitable location or provide the product to the purchaser-licensee.
- The licensor/seller guarantees an income greater than or equal to the price the licensee-buyer pays for the product when it's resold and that there is a market present for the product or service.
- The initial fee paid to the seller in order to start the business opportunity must range between $400 and $1,000.
- The licensor/seller promises to buy back any product purchased by the licensee/buyer in the event it cannot be sold to the prospective customers of the business.

- The licensee/buyer will purchase any products or services developed by the seller/licensor.
- The licensor/seller of the business opportunity will supply a sales or marketing program for the licensee/buyer that many times will include the use of a trade name or trademark.

The laws covering business opportunity ventures usually exclude the sale of an independent business by its owner. Rather, they are meant to cover the multiple sales of distributorships or businesses that do not meet the requirements of a franchise under the Federal Trade Commission (FTC) rule passed in 1979. This act defines business offerings in three formats: package franchises, product franchises and business opportunity ventures.

In order to be a business opportunity venture under the FTC rule, four elements must exist:

- The individual who buys a business opportunity, often referred to as a licensee or franchisee, must distribute or sell goods or services supplied by the licensor or franchisor.

- The licensor or franchisor must help secure a retail outlet or accounts for the goods and services the licensee is distributing or selling.
- There must be a cash transaction between the two parties of at least $500 prior to or within six months after the licensee or franchisee starts the business venture.
- All terms and conditions of the relationship between the licensor and the licensee must be stated in writing.

As you see, the sale of business opportunities as defined by the FTC rule is quite different from the sale of an independent business. When you're dealing with the sale of an independent business, the buyer has no obligations to the seller. Once the sales transaction is completed, the buyer can subscribe to any business operation system he or she prefers. There is no continued relationship required by the seller. Business opportunity ventures, like franchises, are businesses in which the seller makes a commitment of continuing involvement with the buyer.

Types of Business Opportunities

The FTC describes the most common types of business opportunity ventures as follows:

- **Distributorship** – An independent agent enters into an agreement to offer and sell the product of another but is not entitled to use the manufacturer's trade name as part of its trade name. Depending on the agreement, the distributor may be limited to selling only that company's goods or it may have the freedom to market several different product lines or services from various firms.

- **Rack jobber** – A vendor who rents space to sell or display another company's products; this is typically done through a distribution system of racks in a variety of stores that are serviced by the rack jobber. Generally, the agent or buyer enters into an agreement with the parent company to market their goods to various stores by means of strategically located store racks. The parent company obtains a number of locations in which the racks are placed on a consignment basis. It is the agent's responsibility to maintain the inventory, move the merchandise around to attract the customer, and do the bookkeeping. The agent presents the store manager with a copy of the inventory control sheet, which indicates how much merchandise was sold, and then the distributor is paid by the store or location, which has the rack, less the store's commission.

- **Vending machine routes** – The setup is very similar to rack jobbing. The investment however, is usually greater for this type of business venture since the businessperson must buy the machines as well as the merchandise being vended, but here the situation is reversed in terms of the pay procedure. The vending machine operator must pay the location owner a percentage based on sales. The big secret to any route deal is to get locations in high foot-traffic areas, and of course, as close to one another as possible. If your locations are spread far apart, you waste time and traveling expenses servicing them.

In addition to the three types of business opportunities listed above, you should be aware of four other categories:

- **Dealer** – Similar to a distributor but a distributor may sell to a number of dealers, while a dealer will usually sell only to a retailer or the consumer.
- **Network marketing** – This is a generic term that covers the realm of direct sales and multilevel marketing. As a network-marketing agent, you sell products through your own network of friends, neighbors, co-workers etc. In some instances, you may gain additional commissions by recruiting other agents to repeat this process and grow your network or client-base.
- **Trademark/product licenses** – Under this type of arrangement, the licensee obtains the right to use the seller's trade name as well as specific methods, equipment, technology or products. Use of the trade name however, is optional.
- **Cooperatives** – This business is similar to a licensee arrangement in which an existing business, such as a hotel or restaurant, can affiliate with a larger network of similar businesses, often for the sole purpose of promoting through a common identity.

Government Protection for your Venture

The FTC Rule, which has been in effect since the latter part of 1979, has had a broad-ranging impact on the franchise and business opportunity industry and would-be franchisees and licensees. The rule is designed to assure all prospective buyers, of either a franchise or a business opportunity, will receive a full disclosure containing the background information necessary to make informed decisions regarding their investment.

Neither the FTC rule nor state regulations can guarantee freedom from fraud. In spite of the FTC's rule and aggressive action at the state level, there are sellers who seek every possible means to escape regulation. That's why you should pay especially close attention to the FTC disclosure statement presented to you in your particular venture agreement.

It is proper procedure that every prospective buyer of a business opportunity receive the FTC disclosure statement at least 10 business days before signing a binding contract or paying money (or other consideration) to the seller. The 10-business day requirement is minimal. If you meet face-to-face with the licensor or a representative to discuss a proposed sale or purchase of the business opportunity, and if the conversation results in a serious sales presentation, the licensor should provide you with a disclosure document at that time. If you do not receive a FTC disclosure document, don't sign anything or pay out any money, even if claims are made that it is "refundable".

Business Opportunities vs. Franchises

As a rule of thumb, a franchisee receives more support from the parent company, is allowed to use the trademarked name, and is more stringently controlled by the franchisor. Business opportunities, on the other hand, don't receive as much support from the parent company, generally aren't offered the use of a trademarked name, and are independent of the parent company's operational guidelines.

As stated previously, there are numerous forms of business opportunity ventures. Some are even turnkey operations similar to many package-format franchises. These business opportunities provide everything you could possibly need to start a business. They usually help with location selection, provide training, offer support for the licensee's marketing efforts, and supply a complete start-up inventory.

Unlike the package-format franchise however, these types of business opportunities aren't trademarked outlets for the parent company. The company's name, logo and how it's legally operated are left solely to the licensee. Many times the only binding requirement between the seller and the buyer is that they purchase inventory solely through the parent company. Of course, all the specific stipulations will be outlined in your disclosure statement and contract.

The Advantages of a Business Opportunity

- **Lower initial fee than a franchise** – Although the number of low-investment franchises has increased, the fee to get into a business opportunity is still considerably lower. The FTC requires a $500 minimum investment for an opportunity to be considered a business opportunity, but there are many that fall under this set fee, although most average around $2,000 to $3,000.

- **Proven system of operation or product –** Existing systems serve to maximize efficiency and returns and minimize problems. It's simply a matter of passing on experience, which is still the best teacher. Most people like having their hands held occasionally; in this case, during a crisis, the parent company is there to help the licensee over the bumps.

- **Intensive training programs –** In any new business, a lot of time and money are used and even wasted, during the "learning period". A good business venture can greatly decrease or eliminate most of the poor investment decisions made by new businesses through intensive training programs.

- **Better financing options –** Usually, because of its strong financial standing, credit line and contractual agreements, the parent company offering the business opportunity can often arrange better financing than an individual could obtain alone. Financial leverage is a huge consideration in any investment situation.

- **Marketing, advertising and promotion** – Most often, small businesspeople don't spend enough money on advertising. When they do, their efforts are often poorly conceived and/or inconsistent. Many parent companies supply the buyer with printed advertising materials, radio ads, TV promos, etc., which all support a strong marketing plan.

- **Ongoing coaching & advisory support** – Most business opportunity ventures offer support not only through professional training but also through a staff such as lawyers, CPAs, or experts in that particular field who offer business advice at no additional cost.

- **Site selection assistance** – Experts in marketing and site selection choose locations using all the scientific tools available to target consumers. Professional negotiators arrange leases and contracts using the power of a large organization to influence property owners and other important figures to agree to the best terms for you.

- **Purchasing power** – Many times, the parent company's tremendous buying power and special buying techniques can bring products, equipment and outside services to the licensee at a much lower cost than an independent could ever get on their own.

- **No ongoing royalties** – In a business opportunity, unlike in a franchise, there are no ongoing royalties to pay to the seller. The profits are all yours.

Basic Guidelines for Choosing a Business Opportunity

First, you want to make sure your business opportunity of choice complies with all business opportunity statutes in all the states in which you plan to operate. Next, find out if the business opportunity you're interested in provides an offering prospectus to buyers. If it's a business opportunity that falls under the FTC rule, then it's required to disclose specific information to you in writing, this is called a disclosure statement.

A disclosure statement is a document that contains everything there is to know about the business opportunity and the seller's company. It includes the promoter's financial strength, how many operating units there are, and exactly what you're going to be required to pay in total so there are no hidden fees. The purpose of the disclosure statement is to protect the licensee as well as the licensor and to eliminate unscrupulous licensors.

When reviewing a disclosure statement, be aware of the following items:

- **The licensor** – The history of the parent company needs to be detailed. It should include the identity and business experience of any persons affiliated with the licensor, whether the company has been involved in any litigation, whether it or any of the officials in the company have ever declared bankruptcy, other initial payments or payments in total, and any other fees.

- **Obligations of the licensee** – If there are any financing arrangements, they must be stated explicitly. If you are going to be required to buy from a specific supplier, that should be stated up front. The disclosure statement also states what the parent company must provide in terms of equipment, training, ongoing services and a training manual.

- **What the licensor promises to deliver** – This should include whether you're getting an exclusive area or territory. The licensor should identify any trademarks, service marks, trade names, logo types and commercial symbols as well as any patents or copyrights that you're going to be able to use as a licensee.

- **Obligations of the licensee** – This tells you how you will participate in the actual operation of the business opportunity. It has provisions for renewal and termination, repurchase and modification. It also has to list the current licensees and their addresses so you have the opportunity to contact other partners.
- **Financial statements of the company** – This is required in almost every state. It is an audited financial statement prepared by a CPA. There is usually a letter from the accountant indicating the books have been audited and are available for people to study. Any estimates or projections of earnings would also be part of the disclosure statement.

HIDDEN CASH COWS WITHIN THE BEAUTY INDUSTRY

The Beauty Industry is a vast community of people with diverse professional talents; their business services are often multi-layered business opportunities and cross over into various sectors within the industry.

In short, health and beauty franchises fall into several categories. The most common are: hair care, skin care, health & wellness, fashion, fitness centers, massage, tanning, tattoo salons and day spas that offer a number of self-care services.

We live in an image-based society, most people, regardless of their profession, long to look and feel beautiful and healthy. For others in the entertainment industry, most of their business is based on their image and thousands upon thousands of dollars are spent each day in our industry for services to support that need. These are your media professionals, film and TV personalities, models, performers of all kind, business leaders, authors, speakers etc. For that reason, in my opinion businesses in this industry are recession resistant.

Without including the numerous additional image-related businesses within the beauty industry, hair and nail care salons alone account for revenue of roughly $48 billion yearly in the U.S. alone. A few other segments of the industry such as cosmetics and fragrance bring in about $13 billion in yearly revenue. The health and wellness services are estimated at roughly $15 billion and body tanning around $5 billion. The U.S. Department of Labor projects the industry will continue to grow faster than the average rate for other occupations through at least 2018.

If you are innovative and ambitious, there is no limit to your earning potential in this industry. You can choose to work behind the scenes as a make-up artist or clothing designer in the performing arts, media or entertainment field, television shows, movies, plays, fashion shows or perhaps, own your own fitness center, health food store, or full-service salon or day spa. You may desire to develop and distribute beauty products internationally, be a health educator, image consultant to the masses or a celebrity stylist. Maybe you wish to start a product line that promotes natural care for the hair, skin, or body. The list of options is endless.

I've done just about all of the above and managed to grow my business brands in a competitive market while maintaining a central customer-base for over 20+ years! God has richly blessed me over the years to serve as an industry leader and resource to thousands of people; it is truly an honor. Great success has been rooted in my decision to use my gifts to serve others. As a result of that intent, I have always experienced God's grace, favor and blessings over the works of my hands.

In addition to God's blessings, I attribute my longevity in the beauty industry to several things. The top factors being great customer service, building strong business relationships, being highly skilled in my niche, staying relevant, on the cutting edge and knowledgeable of consumer trends.

No matter how successful your business grows, it will always be necessary to learn more about your craft and keep your skills sharp through continuous professional development and educational training in your industry.

The training and skills you need depend on what you decide to do and which sector of the industry you choose to enter. If you want to do hair, pick an accredited hair academy with an excellent reputation. The same goes for make-up, nail art, massage therapy, clothing design etc. Being professionally trained in your area of interest is one way of saying to your consumer, "I'm professionally trained and qualified to provide your service needs with excellence".

LAUNCHING A SMALL BUSINESS

Launching a small business or a "start-up" company can be one of the most exciting things you ever do. It is the ultimate way to express yourself to the world, while providing a much-needed service to people who are waiting to buy what you will offer.

I want to provide you with a few basic start-up tips here, but we will delve more deeply in later pages. If you truly desire to learn everything there is to know about business opportunities, ownership or entrepreneurship, etc., I encourage you to look at my website and participate in one of the many online educational resources or host a business/industry specific workshop in your area.

In the meantime, here are a few restatements of previous concepts in the book and new pointers to keep in mind as you launch your start-up company:

- **Build your business around your skills** – Instead of venturing off into uncharted territory; make sure your business is based on your skill sets and professional knowledge. When your business is built around your own personal expertise, you can eliminate undue cost for additional start-up staff, consultants and other advisory personnel.

- **Advertise** – Inform your family, friends, business contacts and past colleagues about your new business. Call, send emails and blast your new venture on all of your social-media profiles. Often times, your friends and family members can help you spread the word, and past business contacts can introduce your brand to their professional networks. This type of grassroots marketing helps introduce your company to a much larger audience.

- **Take advantage of free marketing** – There are several ways to generate buzz for your business without breaking the bank. Social media is a great way to gain exposure and interact with potential customers. You can also reach out to local media and offer your audience your expertise. Make as many local media contacts as you can and be extremely responsive with their service requests. This can lead them to branding you as the local authority, and ultimately generating a lot of free press for your business.

- **Avoid unnecessary expenses** – Create a budget for all of your start-up needs but look for creative ways to get things done without spending money. You will however, have plenty of business costs, some of which can't be avoided. When options are available, be frugal as doing so in the beginning stages can be the difference between a successful and a failed business.

- **Avoid credit card debt** – There is a smart way and a suicidal way to use credit when starting a business. The cost for computers, office furniture, phones and general supplies can all quickly add up. Instead of purchasing everything at once and putting it all on a credit card, use your company's revenue to finance your expenses. By eliminating the stress and burden of debt, you will increase the chances of creating and maintaining a successful business.

- **Hustle hard** – Hard work is an absolute necessity, but when you are starting a business with little to no capital, you must be prepared to dedicate everything you have into making the business a success. This may mean cold calling, doing customer support, dealing with billing and accounting, and handling every other working part of your business until you are in a financial position to hire help. You will wear many hats and it will require the majority of your time and energy if you are to make things work.

Don't let limited capital prevent you from taking a great idea and running with it. Will it be difficult and will you have some stressful situations? Of course, but this is a normal part of entrepreneurship. Are you up for the challenge?

Your life will change dramatically once you start your own business. It is a huge responsibility as everything depends on what you do. This of course, will affect your everyday life. The impact is even greater if your business involves working from your home. The distinction between work time and personal time can be quite blurry and you may experience family or other conflicts over the use of space for business. Also, if you are not exceptional when it comes to time management, it may be difficult to separate your personal time from the hours you dedicate to your business. Time equals money, so if you are not spending your time in a productive way, producing income, your business may be short-lived.

Until you have grown your business to the place where you have trained staff that handles day-to-day operations, you have no more "days off". You are on duty day-in and day-out because if a problem arises with a client, service, or your facility, it is YOUR problem and it won't go away just because you've closed for the holidays or are on vacation.

The buck now starts and stops with you.

Protect Your Business Concept

Patents, trademarks and copyrights are collectively known as intellectual property and generally refer to the rights associated with intangible knowledge or concepts. Intellectual property may be a concern not only if your business is developing or has developed a product, process, or concept that you are taking to market, but also to protect your business name and identity. First, you'll need to understand the differences, and how to perform patent, copyright, or trademark searches.

- **Patent** – An exclusive right granted to the inventor by the government. The patent gives the inventor (or patent holder, if the patent has been assigned) the right to exclude others from making or using the invention for a select period of time, usually 20 years.

To find out whether someone already has a patent on a product, process or concept you're considering, you can perform a patent search online at the United States Patent and Trademark Office (USPTO) website. If your concept is available to pursue, you will then file a patent application with the USPTO. The patent application can be filed online at the USPTO website. Patent application costs vary by the type of filing.

- **Trademark** – The right to use a specific name, word, phrase, symbol, logo, design, sound or color (or a combination of elements) to identify your products and distinguish them from other products. The name must be sufficiently unique—you cannot obtain trademark rights to a generic term like "computers" or "coffee". A service mark is similar, but refers to the right to use a name to identify the source of services, and distinguish that source from other service providers.

There are different types and levels of searches. You can conduct a free online trademark search on the USPTO website but this will only show existing and abandoned federal trademarks and pending trademark applications that are exact matches to the word or phrase you entered.

"Common law usage" of a name or logo begins as soon as you start using it in commerce (the ™ symbol), but protection for common law marks is limited. In order to register a trademark, you must complete a filing with the USPTO. Pricing is around $375 per paper filing and $325 for electronic filings. Once your registration has been approved, you can begin using the ® symbol.

- **Copyright** – A form of protection provided to authors of original works including literary, dramatic, musical, artistic, and certain other intellectual works. Copyright protection is available both on published and unpublished works, including works transmitted online. You don't necessarily need to register a copyright to have copyright protection. A copyright is secured automatically when you create the work. Using the copyright symbol © along with the year of first publication (or creation for unpublished works), and the author's name signify copyright.

There is no way to perform a copyright search like there is for patents and trademarks; however, in today's world, doing a Google search for particular text or creations will, in many cases show if such a work already exists.

While copyright registration is not necessary, copyright law provides advantages to those who have filed a legal copyright. For example, in order to file a copyright infringement lawsuit in court, registration is necessary. You may file an online copyright with the United States Copyright Office for roughly $35. Paper filings range from $50 to $65.

E- Commerce and Basic Marketing Strategies

The internet has transformed the way small business owners get things done. The revolutionary changes in advertising, e-commerce, and instant communication have transformed business. Whatever business you're doing online, it starts with a domain name or your unique online address. It identifies you and your business, attracts customers, and is the first impression potential customers get of your business. Choosing a good domain name is crucial.

A good business domain name should be:

- **Memorable** – Choose a name that resonates with visitors and will bring them back.
- **Distinct** – Pick something that stands apart from the crowd; not confusing and does not conflict with similar names or businesses.
- **Informative** – Have a name that helps visitors understand what you do or sell.
- **Short** – You don't want a name that will be difficult to remember or type.
- **Intuitive** – Ideally, your name should be one that people would logically assume to be the domain name of your website if searching for it online.

In terms of online marketing strategies, you may want to also:

- **Get multiple domain names** – Domain names are inexpensive. You can use them for sites with uniquely different content to help with search engine rankings. "Park" them in order to keep competitors from registering them. You may also use them as marketing domains and redirect them to your primary website.

- **Use your own name** – In addition to your business name, see if you can use your own name, if you want it to be associated with your business.

- **Get extensions** – I suggest buying at least three main extensions for your website domain. It doesn't cost much and prevents others from competing for site visitors by using your company name. At a minimum, get domain_name.com, .org and .net. Consider other extensions, such as .info, .us, .tv, etc. There are also country specific extensions, such as .ca (Canada); however, some country-specific extensions may require your business to have a physical address in the country.

- **Consider multiple sites** – This is a powerful online marketing tool. Multiple sites can offer identical table fans at different price points, from a single physical address. Multiple sites can hinder search engine optimization efforts, so be sure to weigh the work effort to maintain two sites against the benefits.

For today's businesses, having a great website where customers can find you is essential.

Most customers today research products, services, companies, and potential vendors online prior to purchasing. Additionally, many then make their purchases online. Creating your company's website doesn't need to be expensive, or complicated, but it should be well thought out. Once you've outlined your company's website project, you can act on your content, implementation plans and begin building. There's no substitute for having a site that is attractive, user-friendly, and resourceful for visitors.

Here are a few tips on developing your website's content:

- **Users aren't always "readers"** – Web users typically scan a page first to determine if it's what they want or need. If it is, they'll continue reading. If not, they will go back to the list of search results.
- **Keep it short & sweet** – Even when users find online content interesting, about 80% will only scan a web page for "highlights" and move on.
- **Don't be wordy** – As few as 15% of site visitors actually read the entire contents of a page—all the more reason to parse copy into manageable chunks rather than long articles.

- **Offer unique visuals** – Remember there are many ways to deliver messages—use multimedia videos, audios, and other visual elements like slideshows to be compelling rather than just using text.

SEARCH ENGINE OPTIMIZATION (SEO)

SEO is a core tool for pushing traffic to your website. No matter what kind of business you are in, you want your site to be easily accessible and searchable. It is the key to increasing sales and growing a profitable business.

Search engines look for specific features on millions of different sites to determine how relevant they are to a user performing a search. SEO is the process of optimizing your website so the search engines will find it relevant and display it in the list of search engine results. The higher it appears, the more likely a user is to click and view it.

There are several steps for search engine optimization:

- **Keyword optimization** – Make sure your site contains the right SEO keywords. Research popular keywords related to your site/industry. Make sure your site has content relevant to these terms. Strategically work the keywords into your website's copy, headlines and page titles, but be careful not to make the text less clear or distract from your overall message.

- **Build Links** – Once your site has been optimized for keywords, build inbound links to your site from other more established sites. Search engines consider both inbound links and keywords when determining your search engine rankings.

- **Optimize site technology** – Use language search engines can read, like HTML, to develop your site. Avoid using Flash technology. While Flash may make your site more interesting visually, search engines cannot read this language so they ignore this content.

Your website should make it easy for customers to find and do business with you, whether or not you allow customers to purchase online.

Selecting Your Business's Legal Structure

Whether you've purchased an existing business or are starting a new company, you must first decide which form of organization (or "business entity") is best for you. There are several business types, and each has advantages and disadvantages. Make sure you consult with your attorney or accountant about which type of business is most beneficial for your particular situation before making a final decision.

Let's look at business entity types or legal structures. The standard corporation, or **C Corporation**, is a separate legal entity owned by shareholders. You form the corporation by filing incorporation documents with a state and paying the related filing fees. The corporate structure limits each owner's or shareholder's personal liability for the corporation's business debts to the amount invested in the company by the shareholder.

You may consider a C corporation if you:

- Need venture capital for financing.
- Want flexibility to spread the business earnings between the corporation and shareholders for tax-planning purposes.

- Want flexibility to set salaries for employees/owners to minimize Social Security and Medicare taxes.
- Want flexibility to provide (through the corporation) substantial health and medical benefits and other fringe benefit programs for things like education, life insurance, and transportation costs.
- Want to be able to easily sell your business.
- Want to be able to offer stock options to employees.
- Expect your business to own real estate.
- Prefer to lower your risk of IRS audit exposure, since there is a higher audit rate for business income that is reported solely on Schedule C of Form 1040 (U.S. Individual Income Tax Return).

The next option is an **S corporation**, which is a standard corporation that has elected a special tax status with the IRS. The formation requirements are the same as those for C corporations: The S Corporation's special tax status eliminates the double-taxation that can occur with a C corporation's income. A corporate income tax return is filed, but no tax is paid at the corporate level. Instead, business profits or losses "pass through" to shareholders and are then reported on their individual tax returns. Any tax due is paid by shareholders at their individual tax rates.

You may consider an S corporation if you want:

- To take advantage of benefits this corporate business type holds, but you want to take advantage of pass through taxation.
- Flexibility of accounting methods because corporations must use the accrual method of accounting unless they are considered a small corporation with gross receipts of $5,000,000 or less. S corporations typically don't have to use the accrual method unless they have inventory.
- Flexibility to set salaries for employees and owners and to minimize social security and Medicare taxes.
- Lower risk of IRS audit exposure as S corporations file an informational tax return.

While C corporations and S corporations may seem very similar, there are a few key differences:

- **Taxation** – C corporations are separately taxable entities and file a corporate tax return, reporting profits or losses. Any profits are taxed at the corporate level, and losses don't pass through for use by the shareholders to offset other taxable income. The profits of C corporations face possible double taxation when corporate income is distributed to shareholders as dividends. First, the corporation pays tax on its corporate income; then, the shareholders pay personal income tax on the same income when it is distributed to them as dividends.

Conversely, S corporations pay no taxes at the corporate level. Profits and losses are passed through the corporation and reported on the shareholders individual tax returns.

Here are a few additional differences between S and C corporations you may want to consider:

- **Corporate ownership** – C corporations can have an unlimited number of shareholders, while S corporations are restricted to a max of 100 shareholders. In addition, C corporations can have non-US citizens/residents as shareholders, but S corporations cannot. S corporations cannot be owned by C corporations, other S corporations, LLCs, partnerships, or many trusts. C corporations, on the other hand, are not subject to the same restrictions. S corporations can have only one class of stock, while C corporations can have multiple.

- **S corporation election** – A corporation must elect to become an S corporation by making a timely filing of Form 2553 with the IRS, and all shareholders of the corporation must agree in writing to the S corporation election.
- **Limited Liability Company (LLC)** – This is one of the most common elected legal business structures. It provides an alternative to corporations and partnerships by combining the corporate advantage of limited liability protection with the partnership advantage of pass-through taxation. With this tax status, the LLC's income is not taxed at the entity level; however, the LLC typically completes a partnership return if the LLC has more than one owner. The LLC's income or loss is passed through the LLC and reported on the owners' individual tax returns. Taxes in this case are then paid at the individual level.

    LLCs also have fewer ongoing formalities and obligations than corporations do. You form an LLC by filing incorporation documents with a state and paying the related filing fees.

You may consider an LLC structure if:

- Your startup company anticipates losses for at least two years and you want to be able to pass the losses through to yourself and the other owners.
- You want flexibility for accounting methods as LLCs are not required to use the accrual method of accounting as C corporations typically are.
- You wish to minimize ongoing formalities; unlike corporations, which are required to hold annual meetings of directors and shareholders and keep detailed documents and records for all corporate meetings and major business decisions, LLCs do not face as strict of requirements in this area.
- You want flexibility for sharing profits among owners.
- Your business may own real estate.

Start Up Checklist

Hopefully, at this point you have a better understanding of yourself as a business professional, entrepreneur, or potential business owner. In addition to the start-up checklist I have included in this chapter, there are also additional sample business documents in the back of this book that you may tailor to your specific needs.

	BUSINESS START-UP CHECK LIST
☐	Prepare a business plan that outlines your business goals, operating procedures, competitors, as well as the company's current and desired funding.
☐	Select your business structure and file all mandatory incorporation papers. This step provides the owner(s) with personal asset protection from the debts and liabilities of the company.
☐	Address necessary post-incorporation formalities such as establishing contracts for shared business ownership or operations.
☐	Obtain your federal tax number, also called an employer identification number or EIN. The IRS uses it to identify your business for all taxation matters.
☐	Obtain a state tax identification number. Contact your state's taxation department to determine whether your state of formation imposes this requirement.

BUSINESS START-UP CHECK LIST

☐ Obtain the necessary business licenses and/or permits. Licenses may be required by your city, municipality, county and/or state. Contact your Secretary of State and local government to ensure you meet all requirements.

☐ Select an accountant and attorney to assist with your organizational needs throughout the life of the business.

☐ Open a business bank account. Contact your bank about business banking requirements to ensure you have all the necessary paperwork.

☐ Set up your business accounting/bookkeeping procedures. Be prepared to account for all disbursements, payments received, invoices, accounts receivable/payable, etc.

☐ Establish business credit. A line of credit lessens the number of times your business must prepay for products. It also establishes a favorable credit history.

☐ Obtain business insurance. Discuss your particular industry and business needs with your insurance agent to obtain the appropriate type and amount of insurance.

☐ Ensure you comply with all government operational requirements such as unemployment insurance, worker's compensation, OSHA, payroll tax requirements, self-employment taxes, etc.).

☐ Determine your business location and take these steps:
- Home-based: Check zoning requirements
- Commercial location: Lease office or retail space and obtain the necessary furniture, equipment and supplies.

BUSINESS START-UP CHECK LIST
☐ Create any necessary contracts, service agreements and invoices so you can easily bill customers, track payments and keep records.
☐ Budget all projected expenses. Obtain business financing or seek funding sources such as investors, donors, or grants.
☐ Create a logo, business cards, letterhead, envelopes, etc., to build business identity.
☐ Secure your company's domain name with a registered website.
☐ Create a website. A company website allows you to establish your brand and will be your first opportunity to make an impression on your customers.
☐ Create a marketing plan for your products and services. Increase the likelihood for success with a plan for advertising and promoting your products and services to your target market.

Establishing Business Credit

Establishing business credit is an important step for any new small business and helps you maintain a credit history separate from your personal credit history. By having a separate business credit history, you can minimize the effect negative events one might have on the other. For example, if you had some financial challenges that impacted your personal credit score, they shouldn't necessarily affect your small business credit if you have established a clear separation and vice versa.

Having good business credit can provide a number of benefits, including:

- Positioning your company for more favorable payment terms with new vendors and suppliers.
- Reducing the number of times you will need to prepay for products or services purchased.
- Allowing you to obtain better interest rates and credit terms from lenders and banks.

Once you have established and built good business credit, be sure to monitor and protect it, just as you should with your personal credit.

Select Business Appropriate Insurance

There are different types of business insurance that provide several types of coverage. There is coverage against damages to your business's location, i.e. office, factory, storage etc., as well as property such as vehicles, equipment, and inventory. There is business insurance to protect against losses resulting from crimes, coverage for extended leaves of absence due to illness or protection against theft or even employee fraud.

Additionally, there are many types of business liability insurances, which protect your company in the event of a lawsuit. Business insurance can be divided into four basic categories:

- **Property insurance** – Reimburses any insured party who has suffered a financial loss because property (land, buildings, personal property, etc.) has been damaged or destroyed.

- **Liability insurance** – Delivers protection to pay for bodily injury or property damages when the insured is legally responsible.

- **Business automobile insurance** – Provides protection against damages caused by the vehicles used for business purposes. Similar to personal auto insurance, comprehensive coverage provides compensation for vehicle damages resulting from fire or theft; collision covers losses due to an accident; and liability coverage protects you if you are sued for an accident involving a company vehicle.

- **Business umbrella insurance.** Extends coverage for losses above the limit of another policy or policies. An umbrella policy may also extend coverage for losses not normally covered in the other policy.

Outside of these four basic categories, other types of business insurance coverage includes workers compensation insurance, business interruption insurance, group health insurance, group life insurance and disability insurance.

While insurance does provide a measure of security and is essential for some occupations and activities, it does not shield your assets from all potential threats. Insurance policies are limited in what risks they cover and how much they pay. Moreover, insurance can't adequately protect you from economic downturns and the inability to make payments to creditors.

One of the tried and true ways to protect yourself and your assets against creditors is to structure your business using two entities; a **holding entity** and an **operating entity**. As the names imply, the holding entity holds the title to the business assets, then leases or loans them to the operating entity, which conducts the day-to-day business. Yes, all this does sound complicated. However, if you have a highly successful business or a business that has significant exposure to lawsuits, such as a restaurant or construction company, the initial aggravation and cost will reward you with substantial peace of mind in the long-run.

Compliance and Annual Reporting

Business compliance requirements fall into two categories: internal and external. Internal requirements are actions that must be taken within the corporation or Limited Liability Company by the directors, shareholders, members and other managing executives. Although they are the most commonly overlooked, internal requirements must be documented as part of a company's records. It may be necessary to present these records when selling the company or in the event of a lawsuit.

Many small business owners use compliance kits to organize their records. These include items such as sample bylaws or operating agreements, stock or membership interest certificates, transfer ledger, corporate or LLC seal, and sample meeting minutes.

External requirements are those imposed by the state in which your business is incorporated and any state where it is registered to transact business. State compliance requirements often include an annual state filing or an annual report and payment of corresponding fees.

If a corporation or LLC is sued and unable to show it met all corporate or LLC formalities and state requirements, a judge can rule that the company has been acting more like a sole proprietorship or general partnership. This can result in "piercing the corporate veil" meaning limited liability protection disappears and leaves individual owner(s) assets vulnerable if a lawsuit judgment is made against the company.

There are also consequences on the state level that can happen prior to piercing the corporate veil. If a corporation or LLC does not comply with a state's annual or ongoing requirements, that company is no longer in "good standing." Each state has different parameters for what they deem as good standing and many impose late fees and interest payments on outstanding annual reporting and/or franchise tax fees. Being out of compliance or good standing long enough may lead to administrative dissolution, in which all benefits of being a corporation or LLC are lost.

Business Licenses and Permits

If you're starting your own company, be sure to avoid the common mistake of overlooking the licenses and permits you need to run your business. Nearly all businesses require some form of federal, state or local business licenses. You don't want to start your business off on the wrong foot by failing to obtain your licenses before transacting business.

Federal licenses are typically required only for businesses regulated by a federal agency, such as the Securities and Exchange Commission and the Bureau of Alcohol, Tobacco and Firearms. But there are many different types of state licenses, generally granted by state agencies or the state department of taxation. Most local counties and municipalities require licenses too. Here are some examples:

- Many occupations require a specific amount of certified education and/or training, including doctors, lawyers, accountants, barbers, real estate agents, etc. and therefore require licenses.
- Many states have licensing requirements for bars and restaurants.

- Most retail businesses need a sales tax license.
- On the local (city and/or county) level, most businesses need a general business license to operate in a particular city or county. There are often local tax-related licenses too.

There are a plethora of permits required according to your business location and type. They act as evidence that you are in compliance with local ordinances that govern things such as the appearance of the community and safety to consumers. Here are some examples:

- Health department permits are needed for businesses involved in food preparation.
- Sign permits are used to govern the appearance and/or location of business signs.
- Fire department permits are used to govern the public safety of your business location.

If you operate a home-based business, be sure to check on zoning requirements. Some cities prohibit certain business activities in residential areas. If this is the case for your location, you may be able to petition for a variance, which is an exception, to operate from your home. Check with your city or county zoning office on the zoning ordinances for your neighborhood.

To determine which business licenses may be necessary for your particular business, contact the appropriate state and local agencies to verify your requirements and application procedures.

Adhering to policies and procedures is a central part of being successful in business. As a new business owner, complying with all laws and ordinances governing your type of business and location will prevent you from detouring off the road of success.

Tips for Choosing Your Business Location

Choosing a business location is perhaps the most important decision a small business owner or startup will make, so it requires precise planning and research. It involves looking at demographics, assessing your supply chain, scoping the competition, staying on budget, understanding state laws and taxes, and much more.

Here are some tips to help you choose the right business location.

- **Determine Your Needs** – Most businesses choose a location that provides exposure to customers. Additionally, there are less obvious factors and needs to consider, for example:

- **Brand Image** – Is the location consistent with the image you want to maintain?
- **Competition** – Are the businesses around you complementary or competing?
- **Local Labor Market** – Does the area have potential employees? What will their commute be like?
- **Plan for Future Growth** – If you anticipate further growth, look for a building that has extra space should you need it.
- **Proximity to Suppliers** – They need to be able to find you easily as well.
- **Safety** – Consider the crime rate. Will employees feel safe alone in the building or walking to their vehicles?
- **Zoning Regulations** – These determine whether you can conduct your type of business in certain properties or locations. You can find out how property is zoned by contacting your local planning agency.

Evaluate Your Finances

Besides determining what you can afford, you will need to be aware of other financial considerations:

- **Hidden Costs** – Very few spaces are business ready. Include costs like renovation, decorating, IT system upgrades, and so on.
- **Taxes** – What are the income and sales tax rates for your state? What about property taxes? Could you pay less in taxes by locating your business across a nearby state line?
- **Minimum Wage** – While the current federal minimum wage is $7.25 per hour, many states have a higher minimum. View the Department of Labor's list of minimum wage requirements, which are listed by state.
- **Government Economic Incentives** – Your business location can determine whether you qualify for government economic business programs, such as state-specific small business loans and other financial incentives.

Is the Area Business Friendly?

Understanding laws and regulations imposed on businesses in a particular location is essential. As you look to grow your business, it can be advantageous to work with a small business specialist or counselor. Check what programs and support your state government and local community offer to small businesses. Many states offer online tools to help small business owners start up and succeed. Local community resources such as SBA Offices, Small Business Development Centers, Women's Business Centers and other government-funded programs specifically support small businesses.

Selecting a Dream Team

While some companies start out with just the visionary and a great idea, the company's fate depends, in large part, on the strength of your team. In fact, many venture capitalists say that the character, complementary skill sets and working style of the key players are some of the most important factors in selecting companies in which to invest.

Over the course of my career, I've hired hundreds of people. Some were exceptional employees who were major contributors to our success; others didn't work out. In most cases, when an employee left or was terminated, I was the problem. Those dismissed were good people. I just did not know how to properly hire new employees.

Historically and sadly, the only criteria I used was find the candidate with the best skills, experiences and ability to match a job description.

The C'S of Selecting Great Team Members

1. **Competence**: Does the potential employee have the necessary skills, experiences and education to successfully complete the tasks you need performed?

2. **Capability**: Will this person complete tasks and find ways to deliver on the functions that require more effort and creativity?

3. **Compatibility**: Will this candidate fit well into the culture of your business? Can this person get along with colleagues, and more importantly, can

he or she get along with existing and potential clients and partners?

4. **Commitment Level**: Is the candidate serious about working with the company long term or is he or she simply passing through as they look for "something better"?

5. **Character**: Does the person have core values, morals, and a work ethic that aligns with yours? Are they honest?

Recruiting and Retaining Staff

As all employers quickly learn, there is a world of difference between a worker who is correctly matched to their job and organization, and one who is not. It is essential to the success of your business to match the right people to the right jobs. Here is what you will need to do:

- **Develop accurate job descriptions.** Your first step is to make sure you have an effective job description for each position in your company. Your job descriptions should reflect careful thought as to the roles the individual will fill, the skill sets they will need, the personality attributes that are important to completing their tasks, and any relevant experience that would differentiate one applicant from another. This may sound fairly basic, but you would be surprised at how many small companies fail to develop or maintain updated job descriptions.

- **Create a "success profile"** In addition to creating job descriptions; you should also develop a "success profile" of potential ideal employees for key positions in your company. These persons are the ones who are critical to the execution of your business plan. The list may include such positions as executive team members, project team leaders, district managers and salespeople.

- **Draft the ad** – Describe available positions and the key qualifications required. Although some applicants will ignore these requirements and respond regardless, including this information will help you limit the number of unqualified applicants.

- **Post the ad in the mediums most likely to reach your potential job candidates.** The internet has become the leading venue for posting job openings, but don't overlook targeted industry publications and local newspapers.

- **Develop a series of phone-screening questions** – Compile a list of suitable employment screening questions you can ask over the phone to help you quickly identify the most qualified candidates and eliminate those not qualified.

- **Review the resumes you receive and identify your best candidates** – Once you post your ad, you will start receiving résumés, sometimes many more than you anticipated. Knowing what you're looking for in terms of experience, education and skills will help you weed through these résumés quickly and identify potential candidates.

- **Screen candidates by phone.** Once you've narrowed your stack of résumés to a handful of potential applicants, call the candidates and use your phone-screening questions to further narrow the field. Using a consistent set of questions in both this step and your face-to-face interviews will help ensure you evaluate candidates equally.

- **Select candidates for assessment.** Based on the responses to your phone interviews, select the candidates you feel are best qualified for the next step in your selection process.
- **Assess potential candidates for their skills and attributes using a proven assessment tool** – A résumé and phone interview can only tell you so much about a job applicant. You will need a dependable assessment tool to help you analyze the core behavioral traits and cognitive reasoning speed of your applicants. For example, a good test will provide insights as to whether the individual is conscientious or lackadaisical, introverted or extroverted, agreeable or uncompromising, open to new ideas or close-minded, and emotionally stable or anxious and insecure.

   The success profile you create for each position will help you determine which behavioral traits are important for that position. For example, you would expect a successful salesperson to be extroverted. On the other hand, someone filling a clerical position might be more introverted.

These assessment tests can be administered in person or online. Online testing and submission of results can help you determine whether the applicant should be invited for a personal interview.

- **Schedule and conduct candidate interviews** – Once you've selected candidates using the previous steps, schedule and conduct the interviews. Use a consistent set of 10 to 12 questions to maintain a structured interview and offer a sound basis for comparing applicants.
- **Select the candidates** – Make your selection by matching the best applicant to the profiled job description.
- **Conduct background checks** – This step will uncover any potential problems not revealed by previous testing and interviews.
- **Make an employment offer to the selected candidate** – The information you collected during the interview process will provide you with important insights as to starting compensation levels and training needs.

KNOWING WHEN TO END A BUSINESS RELATIONSHIP

Sometimes in business, you have to make decisions that are unpopular, unpleasant or both. One of the most common scenarios where this is true involves having to bid adieu to a team member or client. Anyone who has ever been in a position where they had to fire someone, or discontinue a working relationship with a popular client, knows how difficult that task can be. When working together it is natural for people to form attachments and friendships. However, sometimes these relationships are unhealthy or prove to be more of a burden than a benefit. You need to not only know how to recognize these damaging relationships but also how to handle them.

Some ways to recognize an unfruitful working relationship are:

- Lack of respect.
- Incomplete assignments.
- Lack of communication.
- Failure to respect boundaries.
- Unrealistic expectations from client.
- No sense of urgency to provide information or complete tasks.

- Client who fails to understand that you have OTHER clients who need your attention.
- Breeched contract that you are unable to resolve amicably.
- You feel stressed just *thinking* about working with that individual.

These are just a few of the things you may experience if you are working with a client or team member who is no longer a benefit to your company. Let's be clear, I'm not talking about normal project aggravation. I'm talking about time, money and resource wasting. If someone is NOT adding to your business, he or she is taking away from it.

Once you decide you need to part ways, always do so in the most professional and respectable manner possible. If you are removing a member of your team, be sure to clearly explain the reasons things didn't work out. Be honest but not accusatory or demeaning.

For example: *"Susan, failing to complete your tasks on time has created delays on this project which hinders progress and upsets our clients. Because of this, I'm afraid that we will no longer be able to work together. I appreciate your efforts and will have any outstanding payments due to you within 2 weeks."* Obviously, different circumstances may require a different approach, but you get the idea.

If you are severing a relationship with a *client,* you may need to follow a more thorough process, especially if there is a contract in place. Put your concerns in writing and be clear that the working relationship has terminated. Note in your correspondence any pending projects, payment arrangements, and establish a timeline for working out any kinks. Let me say this again, PUT EVERYTHING IN WRITING.

By documenting all of the details of the split, you protect yourself and your business. Keep things as civil and respectful as possible as you never know when you might cross paths with this person or their company in the future.

How to end a client relationship is an important social skill to learn. Breaking up affects your credibility, your reputation, and reflects on your business image. Here are some tips on ending a client relationship:

- Be calm. Never be hostile, attack a client, or write a flaming goodbye note or letter.

- Be understanding. Yes, you're splitting up. Be sympathetic that ending a relationship is no easier for the client.
- Be concise. Don't go on and on with explanations. Keep it short, simple, and polite.
- Be professional. Don't drag up past events, point the finger or assign blame. It isn't necessary.
- Be clear. Avoid vague comments. If you're saying goodbye for good, say so.
- Be open. Some people don't realize they're being difficult. Leave room for possible discussion to work out issues.
- Be fair. Don't leave a client stuck with an unfinished project. Offer to complete the work.
- Be reasonable. Leaving a client scrambling to make up for your loss isn't nice. Give notice if you can.
- Be mature. Don't get into a back-and-forth email argument. If you're quitting and there is no going back, don't keep replying to emails that just drag out the situation.
- Be thankful. Every situation teaches us something about ourselves and working with

others. Thank your client for the experience and what you've learned working with him or her.

- Be strong. Many people have a hard time speaking up for themselves and saying no. Gather your courage, and like Nike says, just do it.

It's important to be graceful and polite when you're breaking up with a client. Your business image and reputation depend on it. Make no mistake, bad experiences travel fast and you do not want to be labeled as a difficult or unprofessional person to work with.

MOVING AN EXSISTING BUSINESS TO ANOTHER STATE

Sometimes it is necessary to relocate and companies must move from one state to another. This happens for various reasons, often to lower the cost of doing business or provide a better quality of life for owners and employees. A business move means juggling many tasks: finding suitable space, applying for tax and other incentives (e.g., local property tax abatements), coordinating staff, informing customers, obtaining business licenses, and physically making the move.

Moving a business to another state may feel like starting all over and the start-up steps you take will depend on your business entity, the associated benefits, costs and most importantly, taxes.

Moving a Corporation

If you move your corporate offices to a new state, you have one of three options: 1) continue as a corporation in the old state and register as a foreign corporation doing business in the new state. 2) Dissolve the corporation in the old state and form a corporation in the new state. 3) Do a reorganization, where a corporation is formed in the new state and the old corporation is merged into it. To make your choice, consider the following factors:

- **Ongoing state fees** – If you maintain the old corporation and register to do business in a new state, you must file duplicate annual reports and/or pay franchise taxes. You'll pay a fee to both the old state and the new one.

- **Federal tax issues** – Liquidation may result in income taxes to the corporation and its shareholders. For example, when a C corporation with appreciated assets liquidates, it must recognize income. Shareholders who receive assets upon liquidation also recognize income if their stock has appreciated. Since S corporations are "pass-through" entities, there may be no immediate cost to the corporation or its shareholders.

- **Reorganization** – For a C corporation, this can be entirely tax-free. There is no tax on the merger of the old corporation into the new one. It's as if there had been no change for federal tax purposes, but the merged corporation does cease to exist in its original state.

- **Dissolution costs** – If you dissolve your business, whether it is a C corporation or S corporation and either form a new one or merge it into a new corporation, you must go through the formalities of dissolving the old one. The specifics depend on the state in which you had the old corporation. Generally, it requires document preparation (dissolution papers or forms), a filing with the old state and paying any outstanding taxes and dissolution fees.

Moving an LLC

Limited liability companies that relocate face similar choices to corporations but with more options for handling things organizationally.

- **Continue the LLC** in the old state and register to do business as a foreign LLC in the new state. Doing so means duplicate annual reports and/or franchise tax fees. It can also complicate tax filing and reporting for the LLC and its members.
- **Liquidate the LLC** in the old state and form a LLC in the new state. Liquidating an LLC does not entail any federal tax consequences.

Since the LLC is a pass-through entity, it does not report any gain from liquidation.

- **Form a New LLC** – You can form a new LLC in the new state and have members (owners) continue membership interests from the original LLC.
- **Merge LLCs** – You can form an LLC in the new state and merge the existing LLC into it. This is viewed as a continuation of the old LLC and no new federal EIN is required. There are also no immediate tax consequences, provided LLC members from the old state continue to own at least a 50% interest in the capital and profits of the LLC in the new state.

Ending a Business

For some small business owners, the time comes when they must end operations and dissolve their business. It's a stressful time and a multi-step process.

For corporations or LLCs, the company owners must approve the dissolution of the business. With corporations, the shareholders must approve the action; with LLCs the members grant approval. For small businesses, shareholders or members are often involved in day-to-day operations, and typically know the circumstances.

The bylaws of a corporation and the LLC operating agreement typically outline the dissolution process and needed approvals. To comply with corporation formalities, the board of directors should draft and approve the resolution to dissolve. Shareholders then vote on the director-approved resolution. All actions should be documented and placed in the corporate record book. While LLCs are not subject to the same formalities, documenting the decision and member approval is recommended.

After shareholders or members have voted for the dissolution, paperwork must be filed with the state in which the business was incorporated. If the company was qualified to transact business in other states, paperwork must be filed in those states also.

- The process for filing the Certificate of Dissolution (also called Articles of Dissolution) varies by state. Some states require filing documents before notifying creditors and resolving claims; others require filing after that process.
- Certain states require tax clearance for the company before the Certificate of

Dissolution can be filed. In these cases, any back-taxes owed by the corporation or LLC must first be paid.

- Contact your online incorporator or Secretary of State's office to obtain details for your business type in your state.

Although you're ending operations, your tax obligations do not immediately cease. You must formalize the business closing with the IRS as well as your state and local taxing agencies. The IRS website includes a checklist for closing a business, which indicates the required forms and links to additional state and local requirements. Remember, there are payroll-reporting obligations if you have employees. Be sure to consult your accountant or tax adviser on your particular requirements in this area.

You must notify all of your company's creditors by mail, and explain:

- That your corporation or LLC has been dissolved or has filed the statement of intent to dissolve.
- The mailing address to which creditors must send their claim(s).
- A list of the information that should be included in the claim.

- The deadline for submitting claims (often 120 days from the date of the notice).
- A statement that claims will be barred if not received by the deadline.

Your state may allow for claims from creditors not known to the company at the time of dissolution. You may be required to place a notice in the local paper about your company's dissolution. When in doubt, ask an attorney about what your state mandates in this area.

Creditor claims can be accepted or rejected by your company. Accepted claims must be paid or satisfactory arrangements made with creditors for repayment. For example, a creditor may agree to settle the claim for less (such as 80%) than the original amount. With rejected claims, you must advise creditors in writing that your company rejects their claims. Be sure to have an attorney assist and advise you about the process and your state's related statutes.

After paying claims, remaining assets may be distributed to company owners in proportion to the share of ownership. For example, if you own 80% of the business and your brother owns 20%, you receive 80% of the remaining assets. Distributions must be reported to the IRS. If your corporation has multiple stock classes, corporate bylaws typically outline the procedure for distributing assets to these shareholders. For details on distribution and your ongoing contingent liabilities, contact an accountant or tax adviser.

DON'T STOP NOW, KEEP RISING TO THE TOP!

The reality is, if you are alive, have a creative mind, and are passionate about being successful; you can locate your dream career and fulfill your destiny in business. As you travel on the road to destiny there will be many bumps and bruises along the way; you may fail several times before reaching your goals. You may try several careers before finding out how to best utilize your gifts. You may have five start-up companies to crash before you figure out how to refine your business model in a way that it is productive. What I'm saying is not every day will be sunshiny but temporary dark spots should never cause you to give up on yourself or your dreams.

Keeping sight of your life vision will help you during the hard times to "see" what you may not see physically happening this moment. "Now faith is the substance of things hoped for and the evidence of things not seen" (Hebrews 11:1). No matter what happens, never lose your faith. Faith and vision will be the driving forces that keep you running on your journey. You are already equipped for success; your Creator built you for it, designed you to be fruitful and multiply in every good work!

So even if a business venture fails, that does not mean you are a failure. It just means you are being tested and learning how to become more successful at your next launching of a business goal.

By understanding who you are, what gifts you possess, what you REALLY want in life, and planning to execute your goals strategically, you have completed over 85% of the process of being successful and achieving your goals. Now it is just a matter of working, refining and perfecting the process. Once you do this, you are at a point where your business is productive and operating like a well-oiled machine and you can replicate your model through expansion.

Go forth and prosper! My prayer is that this book has provided you with GUIDANCE FOR YOUR JOURNEY.

CRT

GUIDANCE FOR YOUR JOURNEY

BONUS RESOURCE

PAGES

The excerpts, assessments, and sample contracts in the following pages were gathered from various online business support portals. As such, the referenced page numbers are not found in this book but may be located on the original source documents. All source credits have been provided for your continued research and development.

APPENDIX 1

SAMPLE BUSINESS PLAN (GUIDE) FOR A STARTUP BUSINESS

The business plan consists of a narrative and several financial worksheets. The narrative template is the body of the business plan. It contains more than 150 questions divided into several sections. Work through the sections in any order that you like, except for the Executive Summary, which should be done last. Skip any questions that do not apply to your type of business. When you are finished writing your first draft, you'll have a collection of small essays on the various topics of the business plan. Then you'll want to edit them into a smooth-flowing narrative.

The real value of creating a business plan is not in having the finished product in hand; rather, the value lies in the process of researching and thinking about your business in a systematic way. The act of planning helps you to think things through thoroughly, study and research if you are not sure of the facts, and look at your ideas critically. It takes time now, but avoids costly, perhaps disastrous, mistakes later.

This business plan is a generic model suitable for all types of businesses. However, you should modify it to suit your particular circumstances. Before you begin, review the section titled Refining the Plan, found at the end. It suggests emphasizing certain areas depending upon your type of business (manufacturing, retail, service, etc.). It also has tips for fine-tuning your plan to make an effective presentation to investors or bankers. If this is why you're creating your plan, pay particular attention to your writing style. You will be judged by the quality and appearance of your work as well as by your ideas.

It typically takes several weeks to complete a good plan. Most of that time is spent in research and re-thinking your ideas and assumptions. But then, that's the value of the process. So make time to do the job properly. Those who do never regret the effort.

And finally, be sure to keep detailed notes on your sources of information and on the assumptions underlying your financial data.

If you need assistance with your business plan, contact the SCORE office in your area to set up a business counseling appointment with a SCORE volunteer or send your plan for review to a SCORE counselor at www.score.org. Call 1-800-634-0245 to get the contact information for the SCORE office closest to you.

Business Plan

OWNERS

Your Business Name
Address Line 1
Address Line 2
City, ST ZIP Code
Telephone
Fax
E-Mail

I. Table of Contents

II. Executive Summary

Write this section last.

We suggest that you make it two pages or fewer.

Include everything that you would cover in a five-minute interview.

Explain the fundamentals of the proposed business: What will your product be? Who will your customers be? Who are the owners? What do you think the future holds for your business and your industry?

Make it enthusiastic, professional, complete, and concise.

If applying for a loan, state clearly how much you want, precisely how you are going to use it, and how the money will make your business more profitable, thereby ensuring repayment.

III. General Company Description

What business will you be in? What will you do?

Mission Statement: Many companies have a brief mission statement, usually in 30 words or fewer, explaining their reason for being and their guiding principles. If you want to draft a mission statement, this is a good place to put it in the plan, followed by:

Company Goals and Objectives: Goals are destinations—where you want your business to be. Objectives are progress markers along the way to goal achievement. For example, a goal might be to have a healthy, successful company that is a leader in customer service and that has a loyal customer following. Objectives might be annual sales targets and some specific measures of customer satisfaction.

Business Philosophy: What is important to you in business?

To whom will you market your products? (State it briefly here— you will do a more thorough explanation in the Marketing Plan section).

Describe your industry. Is it a growth industry? What changes do you foresee in the industry, short term and long term? How will your company be poised to take advantage of them?

Describe your most important company strengths and core competencies. What factors will make the company succeed? What do you think your major competitive strengths will be? What background experience, skills, and strengths do you personally bring to this new venture?

Legal form of ownership: Sole proprietor, Partnership, Corporation, Limited liability corporation (LLC)? Why have you selected this form?

IV. Products and Services

Describe in depth your products or services (technical specifications, drawings, photos, sales brochures, and other bulky items belong in Appendices).

What factors will give you competitive advantages or disadvantages? Examples include level of quality or unique or proprietary features.

What are the pricing, fee, or leasing structures of your products or services?

V. Marketing Plan

Market research - Why?

No matter how good your product and your service, the venture cannot succeed without effective marketing. And this begins with careful, systematic research. It is very dangerous to assume that you already know about your intended market. You need to do market research to make sure you're on track. Use the business planning process as your opportunity to uncover data and to question your marketing efforts. Your time will be well spent.

Market research - How?

There are two kinds of market research: primary and secondary. Secondary research means using published information such as industry profiles, trade journals, newspapers, magazines, census data, and demographic profiles. This type of information is available in public libraries, industry associations, chambers of commerce, from vendors who sell to your industry, and from government agencies.

Start with your local library. Most librarians are pleased to guide you through their business data collection. You will be amazed at what is there. There are more online sources than you could possibly use. Your chamber of commerce has good information on the local area. Trade associations and trade publications often have excellent industry-specific data.

Primary research means gathering your own data. For example, you could do your own traffic count at a proposed location, use the yellow pages to identify competitors, and do surveys or focus-group interviews to learn about consumer preferences. Professional market research can be very costly, but there are many books that show small business owners how to do effective research themselves.

In your marketing plan, be as specific as possible; give statistics, numbers, and sources. The marketing plan will be the basis, later on, of the all-important sales projection.

Economics

Facts about your industry:

- What is the total size of your market?

- What percent share of the market will you have? (This is important only if you think you will be a major factor in the market.)

- Current demand in target market.

- Trends in target market—growth trends, trends in consumer preferences, and trends in product development.

- Growth potential and opportunity for a business of your size.

- What barriers to entry do you face in entering this market with your new company? Some typical barriers are:

  o High capital costs

  o High production costs

  o High marketing costs

  o Consumer acceptance and brand recognition

  o Training and skills

  o Unique technology and patents

  o Unions

  o Shipping costs

  o Tariff barriers and quotas

- And of course, how will you overcome the barriers?

- How could the following affect your company?

  o Change in technology

  o Change in government regulations

  o Change in the economy

  o Change in your industry

Product

In the Products and Services section, you described your products and services as you see them. Now describe them from your customers' point of view.

Features and Benefits

List all of your major products or services. For each product or service:

- Describe the most important features. What is special about it?

- Describe the benefits. That is, what will the product do for the customer?

Note the difference between features and benefits, and think about them. For example, a house that gives shelter and lasts a long time is made with certain materials and to a certain design; those are its features. Its benefits include pride of ownership, financial security, providing for the family, and inclusion in a neighborhood. You build features into your product so that you can sell the benefits.

What after-sale services will you give? Some examples are delivery, warranty, service contracts, support, follow-up, and refund policy.

Customers

Identify your targeted customers, their characteristics, and their geographic locations, otherwise known as their demographics.

The description will be completely different depending on whether you plan to sell to other businesses or directly to consumers. If you sell a consumer product, but sell it through a channel of distributors, wholesalers, and retailers, you must carefully analyze both the end consumer and the middleman businesses to which you sell.

You may have more than one customer group. Identify the most important groups. Then, for each customer group, construct what is called a demographic profile:

- Age
- Gender
- Location
- Income level
- Social class and occupation
- Education
- Other (specific to your industry)
- Other (specific to your industry)

For business customers, the demographic factors might be:

- Industry (or portion of an industry)
- Location
- Size of firm
- Quality, technology, and price preferences

- Other (specific to your industry)

- Other (specific to your industry)

Competition

What products and companies will compete with you? List your major competitors:

(Names and addresses)

Will they compete with you across the board, or just for certain products, certain customers, or in certain locations?

Will you have important indirect competitors? (For example, video rental stores compete with theaters, although they are different types of businesses.)

How will your products or services compare with the competition?

Use the Competitive Analysis table below to compare your company with your two most important competitors. In the first column are key competitive factors. Since these vary from one industry to another, you may want to customize the list of factors.

In the column labeled **Me**, state how you honestly think you will stack up in customers' minds. Then check whether you think this factor will be a strength or a weakness for you. Sometimes it is hard to analyze our own weaknesses. Try to be very honest here. Better yet, get some disinterested strangers to assess you. This can be a real eye-opener. And remember that you cannot be all things to all people. In fact, trying to be causes many business failures because efforts become scattered and diluted. You want an honest assessment of your company's strong and weak points.

Now analyze each major competitor. In a few words, state how you think they compare. In the final column, estimate the importance of each competitive factor to the customer.

1 = critical; 5 = not very important.

Table 1: Competitive Analysis

Factor	Me	Strength	Weakness	Competitor A	Competitor B	Importance to Customer
Products						
Price						
Quality						
Selection						
Service						
Reliability						
Stability						
Expertise						
Company Reputation						
Location						
Appearance						
Sales Method						
Credit Policies						

Factor	Me	Strength	Weakness	Competitor A	Competitor B	Importance to Customer
Advertising						
Image						

Now, write a short paragraph stating your competitive advantages and disadvantages.

Niche

Now that you have systematically analyzed your industry, your product, your customers, and the competition, you should have a clear picture of where your company fits into the world.

In one short paragraph, define your niche, your unique corner of the market.

Strategy

Now outline a marketing strategy that is consistent with your niche.

Promotion

How will you get the word out to customers?

Advertising: What media, why, and how often? Why this mix and not some other? Have you identified low-cost methods to get the most out of your promotional budget?

Will you use methods other than paid advertising, such as trade shows, catalogs, dealer incentives, word of mouth (how will you stimulate it?), and network of friends or professionals?

What image do you want to project? How do you want customers to see you?

In addition to advertising, what plans do you have for graphic image support? This includes things like logo design, cards and letterhead, brochures, signage, and interior design (if customers come to your place of business).

Should you have a system to identify repeat customers and then systematically contact them?

Promotional Budget

How much will you spend on the items listed above?

Before startup? (These numbers will go into your startup budget.)

Ongoing? (These numbers will go into your operating plan budget.)

Pricing

Explain your method or methods of setting prices. For most small businesses, having the lowest price is not a good policy. It robs you of needed profit margin; customers may not care as much about price as you think; and large competitors can under price you anyway. Usually you will do better to have average prices and compete on quality and service.

Does your pricing strategy fit with what was revealed in your competitive analysis? Compare your prices with those of the competition. Are they higher, lower, the same? Why?

How important is price as a competitive factor? Do your intended customers really make their purchase decisions mostly on price?

What will be your customer service and credit policies?

Proposed Location

Probably you do not have a precise location picked out yet. This is the time to think about what you want and need in a location. Many startups run successfully from home for a while.

You will describe your physical needs later, in the Operational Plan section. Here, analyze your location criteria as they will affect your customers.

Is your location important to your customers? If yes, how?

If customers come to your place of business:

Is it convenient? Parking? Interior spaces? Not out of the way? Is it consistent with your image?

Is it what customers want and expect?

Where is the competition located? Is it better for you to be near them (like car dealers or fast food restaurants) or distant (like convenience food stores)?

Distribution Channels

How do you sell your products or services? Retail

Direct (mail order, Web, catalog) Wholesale

Your own sales force

Agents

Independent representatives

Bid on contracts

Sales Forecast

Now that you have described your products, services, customers, markets, and marketing plans in detail, it's time to attach some numbers to your plan. Use a sales forecast spreadsheet to prepare a month-by-month projection. The forecast should be based on your historical sales, the marketing strategies that you have just described your market research, and industry data, if available.

You may want to do two forecasts: 1) a "best guess", which is what you really expect, and 2) a "worst case" low estimate that you are confident you can reach no matter what happens.

Remember to keep notes on your research and your assumptions as you build this sales forecast and all subsequent spreadsheets in the plan. This is critical if you are going to present it to funding sources.

VI. Operational Plan

Explain the daily operation of the business, its location, equipment, people, processes, and surrounding environment.

Production

How and where are your products or services produced? Explain your methods of:

- Production techniques and costs

- Quality control

- Customer service

- Inventory control

- Product development

Location

What qualities do you need in a location? Describe the type of location you'll have. Physical requirements:

- Amount of space

- Type of building

- Zoning

- Power and other utilities

Access:

Is it important that your location be convenient to transportation or to suppliers? Do you need easy walk-in access?
What are your requirements for parking and proximity to freeway, airports, railroads, and shipping centers?

Include a drawing or layout of your proposed facility if it is important, as it might be for a manufacturer.

Construction? Most new companies should not sink capital into construction, but if you are planning to build, costs and specifications will be a big part of your plan.

Cost: Estimate your occupation expenses, including rent, but also including maintenance, utilities, insurance, and initial remodeling costs to make the space suit your needs. These numbers will become part of your financial plan.

What will be your business hours?

Legal Environment

Describe the following:

- Licensing and bonding requirements

- Permits

- Health, workplace, or environmental regulations

- Special regulations covering your industry or profession

- Zoning or building code requirements

- Insurance coverage

- Trademarks, copyrights, or patents (pending, existing, or purchased)

Personnel

- Number of employees

- Type of labor (skilled, unskilled, and professional)

- Where and how will you find the right employees?

- Quality of existing staff

- Pay structure

- Training methods and requirements

- Who does which tasks?

- Do you have schedules and written procedures prepared?

- Have you drafted job descriptions for employees? If not, take time to write some.
- They really help internal communications with employees.

- For certain functions, will you use contract workers in addition to employees?

Inventory

- What kind of inventory will you keep: raw materials, supplies, finished goods?

- Average value in stock (i.e., what is your inventory investment)?

- Rate of turnover and how this compares to the industry averages?

- Seasonal buildups?

- Lead-time for ordering?

Suppliers

Identify key suppliers:

- Names and addresses

- Type and amount of inventory furnished

- Credit and delivery policies

- History and reliability

Should you have more than one supplier for critical items (as a backup)?

Do you expect shortages or short-term delivery problems?

Are supply costs steady or fluctuating? If fluctuating, how would you deal with changing costs?

Credit Policies

- Do you plan to sell on credit?

- Do you really need to sell on credit? Is it customary in your industry and expected by your clientele?

- If yes, what policies will you have about who gets credit and how much?

- How will you check the creditworthiness of new applicants?

- What terms will you offer your customers; that is, how much credit and when is payment due?

- Will you offer prompt payment discounts? (Hint: Do this only if it is usual and customary in your industry.)

- Do you know what it will cost you to extend credit? Have you built the costs into your prices?

Managing Your Accounts Receivable

If you do extend credit, you should do an aging at least monthly to track how much of your money is tied up in credit given to customers and to alert you to slow payment problems. A receivables aging looks like the following table:

	Total	Current	30 Days	60 Days	90 Days	Over 90 Days
Accounts Receivable Aging						

You will need a policy for dealing with slow-paying customers:

- When do you make a phone call?

- When do you send a letter?

- When do you get your attorney to threaten?

Managing Your Accounts Payable

You should also age your accounts payable, what you owe to your suppliers. This helps you plan whom to pay and when. Paying too early depletes your cash, but paying late can cost you valuable discounts and can damage your credit. (Hint: If you know you will be late making a payment, call the creditor before the due date.)

Do your proposed vendors offer prompt payment discounts?

A payables aging looks like the following table:

	Total	Current	30 Days	60 Days	90 Days	Over 90 Days
Accounts Payable Aging						

VII. Management and Organization

Who will manage the business on a day-to-day basis? What experience does that person bring to the business? What special or distinctive competencies? Is there a plan for continuation of the business if this person is lost or incapacitated?

If you'll have more than 10 employees, create an organizational chart showing the management hierarchy and who is responsible for key functions.

Include position descriptions for key employees. If you are seeking loans or investors, include resumes of owners and key employees.

Professional and Advisory Support

List the following:

- Board of directors
- Management advisory board
- Attorney
- Accountant
- Insurance agent
- Banker
- Consultant or consultants
- Mentors and key advisors

VIII. Personal Financial Statement

Include personal financial statements for each owner and major stockholder, showing assets and liabilities held outside the business and personal net worth. Owners will often have to draw on personal assets to finance the business, and these statements will show what is available. Bankers and investors usually want this information as well.

IX. Startup Expenses and Capitalization

You will have many start-up expenses before you even begin operating your business. It's important to estimate these expenses accurately and then to plan where you will get sufficient capital. This is a research project, and the more thorough your research efforts, the less chance that you will leave out important expenses or underestimate them.

Even with the best of research, however, opening a new business has a way of costing more than you anticipate. There are two ways to make allowances for surprise expenses. The first is to add a little "padding" to each item in the budget. The problem with that approach, however, is that it destroys the accuracy of your carefully wrought plan. The second approach is to add a separate line item, called contingencies, to account for the unforeseeable. This is the approach we recommend.

Talk to others who have started similar businesses to get a good idea of how much to allow for contingencies. If you cannot get good information, we recommend a rule of thumb that contingencies should equal at least 20 percent of the total of all other start- up expenses.

Explain your research and how you arrived at your forecasts of expenses. Give sources, amounts, and terms of proposed loans. Also explain in detail how much will be contributed by each investor and what percent ownership each will have.

X. Financial Plan

The financial plan consists of a 12-month profit and loss projection, a four-year profit and loss projection (optional), a cash-flow projection, a projected balance sheet, and a break-even calculation. Together they constitute a reasonable estimate of your company's financial future. More important, the process of thinking through the financial plan will improve your insight into the inner financial workings of your company.

12-Month Profit and Loss Projection

Many business owners think of the 12-month profit projection as the centerpiece of their plan. This is where you put it all together in numbers and get an idea of what it will take to make a profit and be successful.

Your sales projections will come from a sales forecast in which you forecast sales, cost of goods sold, expenses, and profit month-by-month for one year.

A narrative explaining the major assumptions used to estimate company income and expenses should accompany Profit projections.

Research Notes: Keep careful notes on your research and assumptions, so that you can explain them later if necessary, and so that you can go back to your sources when it's time to revise your plan.

Three-Year Profit Projection (Optional)

The 12-month projection is the heart of your financial plan. 3-year profit projection is for those who want to carry their forecasts beyond the first year.

Of course, keep notes of your key assumptions, especially about things that you expect will change dramatically after the first year.

Projected Cash Flow

If the profit projection is the heart of your business plan, cash flow is the blood. Businesses fail because they cannot pay their bills. Every part of your business plan is important, but none of it means a thing if you run out of cash.

The point of this worksheet is to plan how much you need before startup, for preliminary expenses, operating expenses, and reserves. You should keep updating it and using it afterward. It will enable you to foresee shortages in time to do something about them—perhaps cut expenses, or perhaps negotiate a loan. But foremost, you shouldn't be taken by surprise.

There is no great trick to preparing it: The cash flow projection is just a forward look at your checking account.

For each item, determine when you actually expect to receive cash (for sales) or when you will actually have to write a check (for expense items).

You should track essential operating data, which is not necessarily part of cash flow but allows you to track items that have a heavy impact on cash flow, such as sales and inventory purchases.

You should also track cash outlays prior to opening in a pre-startup column. You should have already researched those for your startup expenses plan.

Your cash flow will show you whether your working capital is adequate. Clearly, if your projected cash balance ever goes negative, you will need more start-up capital. This plan will also predict just when and how much you will need to borrow.

Explain your major assumptions; especially those that make the cash flow differ from the Profit and Loss Projection. For example, if you make a sale in month one, when do you actually collect the cash? When you buy inventory or materials, do you pay in advance, upon delivery, or much later? How will this affect cash flow?

Are some expenses payable in advance? When?

Are there irregular expenses, such as quarterly tax payments, maintenance and repairs, or seasonal inventory buildup that should be budgeted?

Loan payments, equipment purchases, and owner's draws usually do not show on profit and loss statements but definitely do take cash out. Be sure to include them.

And of course, depreciation does not appear in the cash flow at all because you never write a check for it.

Opening Day Balance Sheet

A balance sheet is one of the fundamental financial reports that any business needs for reporting and financial management. A balance sheet shows what items of value are held by the company (assets), and what its debts are (liabilities). When liabilities are subtracted from assets, the remainder is owners' equity.

Use a startup expenses and capitalization spreadsheet as a guide to preparing a balance sheet as of opening day. Then detail how you calculated the account balances on your opening day balance sheet.

Optional: Some people want to add a projected balance sheet showing the estimated financial position of the company at the end of the first year. This is especially useful when selling your proposal to investors.

Break-Even Analysis

A break-even analysis details the sales volume, at a given price, required to recover total costs. In other words, the sales level is the dividing line between operating at a loss and operating at a profit.

Expressed as a formula, break-even is:

Break-Even Sales = Fixed Costs

1- Variable Costs

(Where fixed costs are expressed in dollars, but variable costs are expressed as a percent of total sales.)

Include all assumptions upon which your break-even calculation is based.

XI. Appendices

Include details and studies used in your business plan; for example:

- Brochures and advertising materials

- Industry studies

- Blueprints and plans

- Maps and photos of location

- Magazine or other articles

- Detailed lists of equipment owned or to be purchased

- Copies of leases and contracts

- Letters of support from future customers

- Any other materials needed to support the assumptions in this plan

- Market research studies

- List of assets available as collateral for a loan

XII. Refining the Plan

The generic business plan presented above should be modified to suit your specific type of business and the audience for which the plan is written.

For Raising Capital

For Bankers

- Bankers want assurance of orderly repayment. If you intend using this plan to present to lenders, include:

  o Amount of loan

  o How the funds will be used

  o What this will accomplish—how will it make the business stronger?

  o Requested repayment terms (number of years to repay). You will probably not have much negotiating room on interest rate but may be able to negotiate a longer repayment term, which will help cash flow.

  o Collateral offered, and a list of all existing liens against collateral

For Investors

- Investors have a different perspective. They are looking for dramatic growth, and they expect to share in the rewards:

  o Funds needed short-term

  o Funds needed in two to five years

  o How the company will use the funds, and what this will accomplish for growth.

     o   Estimated return on investment

     o   Exit strategy for investors (buyback, sale, or IPO)

     o   Percent of ownership that you will give up to investors

     o   Milestones or conditions that you will accept

     o   Financial reporting to be provided

     o   Involvement of investors on the board or in management

For Type of Business

Manufacturing

- Planned production levels

- Anticipated levels of direct production costs and indirect (overhead) costs—how do these compare to industry averages (if available)?

- Prices per product line

- Gross profit margin, overall and for each product line

- Production/capacity limits of planned physical plant

- Production/capacity limits of equipment

- Purchasing and inventory management procedures

- New products under development or anticipated to come online after startup

Service Businesses

- Service businesses sell intangible products. They are usually more flexible than other types of businesses, but they also have higher labor costs and generally very little in fixed assets.

- What are the key competitive factors in this industry?

- Your prices

- Methods used to set prices

- System of production management

- Quality control procedures. Standard or accepted industry quality standards.

- How will you measure labor productivity?

- Percent of work subcontracted to other firms. Will you make a profit on subcontracting?

- Credit, payment, and collections policies and procedures

- Strategy for keeping client base

High Technology Companies

- Economic outlook for the industry

- Will the company have information systems in place to manage rapidly changing prices, costs, and markets?

- Will you be on the cutting edge with your products and services?

- What is the status of research and development? And what is required to:

- o Bring product/service to market?

- o Keep the company competitive?

- How does the company:

- o Protect intellectual property?

- o Avoid technological obsolescence?

- o Supply necessary capital?

- o Retain key personnel?

High-tech companies sometimes have to operate for a long time without profits and sometimes even without sales. If this fits your situation, a banker probably will not want to lend to you. Venture capitalists may invest, but your story must be very good. You must do longer-term financial forecasts to show when profit take-off is expected to occur. And your assumptions must be well documented and well argued.

Retail Business

- Company image

- Pricing:

- o Explain markup policies.

- o Prices should be profitable, competitive, and in accordance with company image.

- Inventory:

- o Selection and price should be consistent with company image.

- o Inventory level: Find industry average numbers for annual inventory turnover rate (available in RMA book). Multiply your initial inventory investment by the average turnover rate. The result should be at least equal to your projected first year's cost of goods sold. If it is not, you may not have enough budgeted for startup inventory.

- Customer service policies: These should be competitive and in accord with company image.

- Location: Does it give the exposure that you need? Is it convenient for customers? Is it consistent with company image?

- Promotion: Methods used, cost. Does it project a consistent company image?

- Credit: Do you extend credit to customers? If yes, do you really need to, and do you factor the cost into prices?

APPENDIX 2

SAMPLE BUSINESS PLAN TEMPLATE

<<COMPANY LOGO>>

<<COMPANY NAME>>
BUSINESS PLAN

<<Prepared by: _____>>

<<Date>>

Table of Contents   Page

Confidentiality Agreement

The undersigned reader acknowledges that the information provided in this business plan is confidential; therefore, the reader agrees not to disclose it without the express written permission of <<Company/Promoter>>.

It is acknowledged by the reader that information to be furnished in this business plan is in all respects confidential in nature, other than information that is in the public domain through other means, and that any disclosure or use of this confidential information by the reader may cause serious harm or damage to <<Company>>.

Upon request, this document is to be immediately returned to <<Company/Promoter>>.

_____

Signature

_____

Name (printed)

_____

Date

This is a business plan. It does not imply offering of securities.

1. Executive Summary

<< Introduce promoters here, and the reason you are now preparing this Business Plan.

This section should not be completed until the business plan is written. It will highlight all milestones in the company's development over the next five years. It should sum up the following areas:

- Purpose of the plan
- Product or service and its advantages
- Market opportunity
- Management team
- Track record, if any
- Financial projections
- Funding requirements

Financial projections should be summarized and highlighted. The following format is suggested as a guide:

	Year 1	Year 2	Year 3
Sales			
Exports			
Net Profit before Tax			
Investment			
Employment			

! Remember that potential investors often make a provisional judgment based on the executive summary, and that their decision to read the main body of the business plan will depend on the information presented here. The appendices at the back of the plan contain more detailed information to support the main text of the business plan. >>

2. Company Description

Promoters and Shareholders

<< Description of the people involved in starting the business:

- Promoters
- Management structure and areas of responsibility
- Shareholders names, no. of shares, % shareholding and cash investment to date

Advisors

<< Financial, legal, and other advisors should be listed, with names, addresses and contact details. >>

Products and services

<< Explain clearly what your product or service is and what it does.

- Background to its development
- Benefits and Features
- Unique selling points
- Advantages to customers
- Disadvantages or weak points
- Future developments >>

Long Term Aim of the Business

<< State the long-term aim of the new business. >>

Objectives

<< State the specific milestones to be achieved by the company over the next five years (sales, exports, employment, product development, etc). >>

SWOT Analysis

<< Analyze the strengths and weaknesses of the business and product or service, the opportunities that exist in the marketplace, and the threats to the viability of the project. This is best done in a matrix diagram as follows:

Strengths	Weaknesses
•	•
•	•
Opportunities	**Threats**
•	•
•	•

3. Market Analysis

<< This section covers market research and competitor analysis. You must show that you have done the market research to justify the projections made in your business plan. It must demonstrate that there is a viable market and that you can beat the competition in the market for sales. >>

Target Market

<< The market to which you are planning to sell the product or service. Analyze the segments of this market as follows:

- Size of each market segment
- Is the segment growing or declining?
- Characteristics of potential customers in each segment
>>

Total Market Valuation

<< Show the total potential value of the market for this type of product or service, in all the targeted markets, domestic and international. >>

Target Company Revenue

<< These figures are the basis for the sales figures in your financial projections and must be based on realistic assessments. Include average deal size, length of sales cycle, recurring revenues>>

Market Trends

<< Analyze what is happening in the market:

- Recent changes
- Future predictions
- Drivers such as demographic changes, economic and legislative factors
- Implications for your product or service

- Your plans to meet future demands and changes in the market >>

Profile of Competitors

<<Analysis of your competitors in the market:

- What are the competing products and services?
- Profile of key players (company size, turnover, profitability etc.) and their market share
- Advantages and disadvantages of the competitors' offerings >>

Competitive Advantage

<< This is your assessment of why potential customers will choose to buy your product in place of those profiled above. Advantages may include:
- Unique features
- Price
- New technologies or systems
- Better value to customers in terms of efficiency or ROI or cost/benefit ratios
- Greater compatibility with existing systems
- Include any independent validation or case studies >>

Benefits to Clients

<< This is what your product or service provides to potential customers in terms of their own business goals. Does your product or service enable them to:

- Increase sales
- Increase efficiencies
- Save money
- Save time
- Maximize resources
- Reduce errors
- Reduce downtime

- Improve Customer Service, reduce churn, increase loyalty

What will buying your product or service actually do for the customer? >>

4. Marketing/Sales Strategy

<< This section sets out your strategies for reaching your target market, arousing their interest in your product or service, and actually delivering the product or service to them in sales. >>

Marketing Strategy

<< How you will position your product or service in the market and differentiate it from its competitors:

- Which segments of the market will be targeted first and why?
- How will this be developed to reach the full target market?
- How will you differentiate your product or service?
- What key benefits will be highlighted?
- What potential customers have you already targeted?
- Have you a test site in operation, and what feedback is coming from this?
- What contacts can be used to generate market awareness and sales?
- Who will do the marketing: staff, agency, reps? >>

Revenue Sources

<< What contributions to revenue and profit will your business have?

	Irl	EU	US	Rest of World
Products				
Services				
Licences				
After sales				
Upgrades				

Sales Strategy

<< How you will sell your product or service to the target market.

- Directly
- Retail
- Distributor
- Agent
- Sales rep
- Website
- Revenue Sharing Partners

Analyze for each method the costs involved, whether it will reach the intended market efficiently, the control you would retain over the pricing and positioning, the logistics, and the overall integration with your marketing strategy. State the advantages of the methods you have chosen to sell your product or service. >>

Pricing

<< How you will set the price charged for your product or service. Considerations include:

- Competitors' prices
- Level of competition in the market
- Perception of quality-price relationship by customers
- Production costs and overheads
- Chain of distribution and the added-value at each stage
- The extent to which the buyer can control the price

State how each product or service will be priced, referring to the income sources above. >>

Marketing and Communications Strategy

<< How you will promote your product or service in the marketplace.

- Advertising – where, when, how, to whom
- Public relations
- Direct marketing
- Website and internet marketing
- Exhibitions and conferences
- Word of mouth >>

5. Research and Development

Technology Roadmap

<< Show the intended future development of your product or service, i.e., changes to meet future market demands, adaptations to international markets, or upgrades. Also detail plans for new products or services to add to the range.

Include

- Team/Department structure
- Methodology
- Platforms used
- Milestones to be achieved
- System Overview Diagram>>

Research and Development

<< Indicate whether you will have ongoing R&D as an activity of the company, what areas this will be exploring and what future contributions to the company you expect from this research. >>

Technical Partners

<< List all partners and indicate nature of involvement >>

IP, Patents, Copyrights, Brands

<< Indicate any protection available for your product or service: whether the technology can be or has been patented, whether you can avail of copyright or trademark registration, and the brand image you intend to build up as a protection against competition. >>

6. Staffing and Operations

<< This is where you will outline the intended structure of the company in terms of management, number of employees, and the physical operational requirements to produce or supply the product or service. >>

Management (including Board) Organization Chart

<< Include a diagram of the way in which the management of the new venture will be organized. This should show the areas of responsibility of each manager and the employees to be taken on over the next three years. >>

Staffing

<< State what employees will be taken on over the next three years, with which skills, in which areas of the business. >>

Training Plans

<< Outline the planned employee and management development to be undertaken in order to maintain a skilled workforce. This should also tie in with the future market developments and any new product or service developments. >>

Operations

<< State the physical requirements of the business:

- Premises
- Equipment
- Production facilities
- Infrastructure
- Communications facilities
- Costs involved
- Suppliers >>

7. Financial Projections

I Key Assumptions   p

II Profit and Loss Accounts   p

III Balance Sheets   p

IV Cash flow   p

Requirements for Preparation of Projections

1. Opening figures included based on latest Mgmt/Audited accounts.

2. Shareholders Fund analyzed into Share Capital, Share Premium and Retained Profits.

3. Sales Assumptions provided by unit, price segment & geography and reconciled to pipeline.

4. Expenditure categorized into R&D, Admin and Overheads and Promoters / key managers salaries.

5. Identification of monthly and cumulative company operational deficits.

6. Sensitivity analysis may be required, detailing strategies to be implemented if sales or expenditure targets are not met.

7. Projections should identify separately Operational Cash Flow and external Cash Injections.

I. Key Assumptions

<< This section reviews the key assumptions used in the financial projections. It is a guide to explain how key figures in the financial projections were arrived at. Included here should be items such as:

- Income sources
- Number of employees projected for each year and their intended salaries
- Projected investment in equipment and materials
- Projected R&D costs
- Depreciation allowed for
- Expected rent and rates charges
- Creditor days expected and debtor days allowed
- Expense calculations

This section should be brief and to the point. Further detail regarding these items can be placed in the Appendices. >>

II. Profit & Loss Accounts

<< Attach here projected profit and loss accounts for the first three years of the company's operations. >>

III. Balance Sheets

<< Attach here projected balance sheets for the first three years
of the company's operations. >>

IV. Cash flow

<< Attach here a monthly cash flow prediction for the first two years of the company's operations. >>

8. Sales Pipeline

Table as follows:

Name of Customer	Size of Deal	Date PO expected	Probability % of Getting Sale

9. Funding Requirements

<< State here the total funding requirements of the business, and how those are intended to be provided. You will also need to state the approximate breakdown of how these funds are to be spent.

Sources:

- Promoters' funds
- Bank lending
- Grants or loans from agencies
- Investment already received
- Investment sought

Required for:

- Equipment
- General Operational Costs
- Marketing
- Staffing >>

10. Appendices

<< This section is used to provide the detailed data on which the main text of the business plan is based, and to provide extra information of interest to the readers of the business plan. Items for inclusion in appendices vary from business to business, but normally include some of the following:

- Promoters' CVs
- Detailed financial assumptions
- Most recent Company Audited Accounts
- Share Cap table and Investment history
- Term Sheet from Potential Investors
- Detailed market research findings
- Promotional literature
- Product or service information
- Details of company website, Social media info
- Testimonials or letters of intent from customers >>

SPIRITUAL GIFTS TEST

God has blessed each believer with Spiritual Gifts. Do you know what Spiritual Gifts God has given you? This Spiritual Gifts Test will help you determine what Spiritual Gift(s) and/or Special Talent(s) God has given you. The test evaluates 28 Gifts and Talents. Do NOT look ahead to see what these Gifts and Talents are because that will influence your results!

Instructions:

This Spiritual Gifts Test consists of 140 statements (pages 2-5) that you are to respond to by entering in a number for each on the Analysis Sheet (page 7). Depending on how you feel about each statement, enter a number between 1 and 10 where 1 means that the statement does not describe you at all and 10 means that the statement describes you perfectly.

This test is designed for Christians. If you have been a Christian for at least a few years, you should use your personal experiences as the basis for your Responses. If you consider yourself to be a new Christian, then your Responses should be based on how well each statement describes the desire of your heart (even if you have not yet done what the statement talks about).

Please keep in mind that this test was written by people, not by God, and as such it is certainly imperfect. It should be used as a starting place to begin to discover how God has gifted you, but not as an absolute indicator. The test may not always indicate your true Spiritual Gift(s). It is just one tool in what should be a life-long search for how God has blessed you so you can bless others.

Read this VERY CAREFULLY!

1. Before you start the test, find the Analysis Sheet (page 7) and fold it along the gray line that runs down the middle of the sheet. Fold it so that you can see the 140 numbered boxes, but cannot see the names of the Spiritual Gifts and Talents.

2. Place the five Test pages (pages 2-6) on top of the folded Analysis Sheet so that you can see the Response 1-28 column.

3. As you take the Test, enter a Response (number from 1 to 10 indicating how well the statement describes you) in each of the pre-numbered boxes.

4. After entering your Responses in the boxes numbered 1-28, flip to the second Test page and position it over the Analysis Sheet so that it covers up the column of Responses you just entered.

5. Now enter your Responses for this page of the test.

6. Continue this process for all five Test pages. The test will take about an hour to complete.

7. Respond to each Statement quickly with your first feeling. Don't be too modest, however, unless you can walk on water, you will probably have many more low number Responses than high number Responses.

8. Are you ready to start? Take a deep breath and begin . . .

9. When you are done, read the Analysis Instructions on page 8.

1. People come to me when they need help in desperate situations, and I am able to recommend a ministry that can help.

2. I feel empowered to stand-alone for Christ in a hostile, unbelieving environment.

3. I readily identify with Paul's desire for others to be single as he was.

4. I enjoy using my artistic talents to make things that bring glory to God.

5. It is easy to me to perceive whether a person is honest or dishonest.

6. I have spoken words of hope that God confirmed in others by the Holy Spirit.

7. I am attracted to non-believers because of my desire to win them to Christ.

8. I have urged others to seek Biblical solutions to their affliction or suffering.

9. I hold fast to my personal belief in the truth even in the presence of ridicule, apparent failure, or pain.

10. I can give sacrificially because I know that God will meet my needs.

11. I feel strongly that my prayers for a sick person effect wholeness for that person.

12. When I serve the Lord, I really don't care who gets the credit.

13. Our home is always open to whomever God brings to us.

14. I find myself praying when I possibly should be doing other things.

15. I have had insights of spiritual truth that others have said helped bring them closer to God.

16. Others are willing to follow my guidance to accomplish tasks for our church.

17. I feel great compassion for the problems of others.

18. I believe that God can miraculously alter circumstances.

19. I am able to relate well to people of different cultures.

20. Christian music always lifts my spirit and makes me want to praise and worship God.

21. I have a heart to help Christians who have lost their way.

22. I choose to live a simple lifestyle so I will have more time and money to devote to God's service.

23. I sometimes feel that I know exactly what God wants to do in a ministry at a specific point in time.

24. Studying the Bible and sharing my insights with others is very satisfying for me.

25. I have interpreted tongues so as to help others worship God without confusion.

26. Sometimes when I pray, it seems as if the Spirit steps in and prays in words I cannot understand.

27. I have felt an unusual presence of God and personal confidence when important decisions needed to be made.

28. Sometimes, I express my love for God by writing poems, songs, prayers, or devotionals.

29. I have been responsible for guiding tasks in my church to success.

30. I feel God has called me to go forth to establish new churches where people have never heard the gospel.

31. I am single and enjoy it.

32. I like to make gifts for others that will remind them of God or Jesus.

33. I can sense whether a person is moved by the Holy Spirit, an evil spirit, or by their own flesh.

34. It is a joy to speak uplifting words to people who are discouraged.

35. I have led others to a decision for salvation through faith in Christ.

36. I can challenge others without making them feel condemned.

37. I am totally convinced God will fulfill his word even if He is not doing so yet.

38. God has used me to meet someone's financial or material need.

39. When I pray for the sick, either they or I feel sensations of tingling or warmth.

40. The Spirit sometimes leads me to do a simple thing for someone that touches him or her deeply.

41. I enjoy greeting and welcoming people to our church or our home.

42. I seem to recognize prayer needs before others.

43. I am able to understand difficult portions of God's word.

44. I am able to delegate tasks to others to accomplish God's work.

45. I have a desire to work with those who have physical or mental problems to alleviate their suffering.

46. Others can point to specific instances where my prayers have resulted in what seems impossible happening.

47. I would be willing to leave comfortable surroundings if it would enable me to share Christ with more people.

48. Singing, dancing to, or playing songs of praise to God for pure enjoyment is personally satisfying.

49. God has shown fruit in my life in the effective discipling of other believers.

50. My desire for spiritual riches always outweighs my desire for money or material possessions.

51. I sometimes have a strong sense of what God wants to say to people in response to particular situations.

52. People have told me that I have helped them learn Biblical truths.

53. Sometimes when a person speaks in tongues, I get an idea about what God is saying.

54. I can speak to God in a language I have never learned.

55. Sometimes God gives me an insight into the proper course of action others should take.

56. I am able to take complex spiritual matters and write them down in a way that others can understand more easily.

57. I can serve others by organizing and harnessing their gifts to solve a particular problem.

58. I have little fear in leading people where God wants them to go.

59. I am glad I have more time to serve the Lord because I am single.

60. I like to work with my hands to make things to serve God.

61. The difference between truth and error is easily perceived by me.

62. I can effectively motivate people to get involved in ministry

63. I seem able to determine when the Spirit has prepared a person to received Jesus Christ.

64. People will take correction from me because they know I am on their side.

65. My hope in God, against all odds, is inspiring to others.

66. I have been willing to maintain a lower standard of living in order to benefit God's work.

67. I enjoy praying for sick people because I know that many of them will be healed as a result.

68. I have enjoyed doing routine tasks that have led to more effective ministry by others.

69. I try to make everyone feel welcome and comfortable at church suppers or social events.

70. When I hear a prayer request, I pray for that need for several days at least.

71. Through study or experience I have discerned major strategies God seems to use in furthering His kingdom.

72. God has given me an ability to "rally the troops" in giving aid to others.

73. I enjoy spending time with a lonely shut-in person or someone in prison.

74. God has used me personally to perform supernatural signs and wonders.

75. The thought of beginning a new church in a new community is exciting to me.

76. People have said they see the love of Jesus on my face when I sing, dance, or play music.

77. I feel that I am responsible to help protect weak Christians from dangerous influences.

78. A big house, a fancy car, or a large bank account are NOT important to me.

79. Sometimes I have a burning desire to speak God's word even if I know it will not be well received.

80. Teaching a Bible Class is one of the most enjoyable things I do (or could do).

81. When others have prayed in tongues, I felt that I understood the meaning of their prayer.

82. Praying in tongues has been meaningful to me in my personal prayer life.

83. When a person has a problem I can frequently guide him or her to the best Biblical solution.

84. I love to study God's Word and write down what I have learned.

85. I can recognize talents and gifts in others, and find ways of using these for God.

86. God has given me a position of authority over a number of groups of Christians.

87. I am single and have little difficulty controlling my sexual desires.

88. I am able to show the glory of God's creation through my art.

89. I can judge well between the truthfulness and error of a given theological statement.

90. I have verbally given confidence to the wavering, the troubled, or the discouraged.

91. I minister better to the spiritually unborn than to believers.

92. It is enjoyable to motivate people to a higher spiritual commitment.

93. I am ready to try the impossible because I have a great trust in God.

94. I have strongly sensed the Spirit leading me to give money to a specific person or cause.

95. Sometimes I have a strong sense that God wants to heal someone through my prayers or words.

96. I would rather work in secret than have my work recognized publicly.

97. I do NOT feel uncomfortable when people drop in unexpected.

98. Praying for others is one of my favorite ways of spending time.

99. I sometimes find I know things that I have never learned, which are confirmed by mature believers.

100. It is a thrill to inspire others to greater involvement in church work.

101. I enjoy visiting in hospitals and retirement homes, and feel I do well in such a ministry.

102. The Holy Spirit leads me to pray for impossible things that really come true.

103. More than most, I have had a strong desire to see peoples of other countries won to the Lord.

104. People have told me they were moved spiritually by my singing, dancing, or playing music.

105. I feel a call from God to be the spiritual leader of a group of Christians.

106. I am NOT jealous of those who have more material possessions than I do.

107. People have told me that I have communicated timely messages that must have come directly from the Lord.

108. I devote considerable time to learning new Biblical truths in order to communicate them to others.

109. When I hear others speak in tongues, I am compelled to explain the meaning.

110. When I give a public message in tongues, I expect it to be interpreted.

111. I feel that I have a special insight in selecting the best alternative in a difficult situation.

112. People say they have been touched spiritually by things I have written.

113. People sometimes look to me for guidance in coordination, organization, and ministry opportunities.

114. God has used me to bring the gospel to people who have never heard.

115. I am single and feel indifferent toward being married.

116. I feel compelled to use my hands to craft things that show the beauty of God's creation.

117. I can quickly recognize whether or not a person's teaching is consistent with God's word.

118. People who are feeling perplexed sometimes come to me for comfort.

119. I'm troubled when salvation is not emphasized.

120. I can identify with weakness and temptation so as to encourage people to repent and believe.

121. I have believed God for the impossible and seen it happen in a tangible way.

122. I strive to find ways to give to others without calling attention to myself.

123. I have prayed for others and physical healing has actually occurred.

124. If someone is facing a serious crisis, I enjoy the opportunity to help them.

125. When people come to our home, they often say they feel at home with us.

126. Others have told me that my prayers for them have been answered in tangible ways.

127. God has given me words to say in witnessing situations that surprised even me.

128. I can motivate others to obey Christ by the living testimony of my life.

129. Sometimes I am overcome with emotion for the person I am praying for.

130. People have told me that I was God's instrument to bring supernatural change in lives or circumstances.

131. People of a different race or culture have been attracted to me, and we have related well.

132. I enjoy using my musical talents to sing, dance to, or play Christian music much more so than secular music.

133. God has given me the ability to teach and preach spiritual truth.

134. I feel that I can best fulfill God's calling on my life by living simply.

135. Through God I have revealed specific things that will happen in the future.

136. I feel I can communicate Biblical truths to others and see resulting changes in knowledge, values, or conduct.

137. My interpretation of tongues has been confirmed by mature believers.

138. When I speak in tongues, I believe it is edifying to the group I am with.

139. People with spiritual problems seem to come to me for advice and counsel.

140. I sometimes prefer to write down my thoughts about God rather than speaking them out loud.

Spiritual Gifts Test - Analysis Sheet

Response 113-140 Enter 1 - 10	Response 85-112 Enter 1 - 10	Response 57-84 Enter 1 -10	Response 29-56 Enter 1 - 10	Response 1-28 Enter 1 - 10		Sum of first 5 columns	Rank in order highest to lowest	Name of Spiritual Gift / Talent
113	85	57	29	1				Administration / Guidance
114	86	58	30	2				Apostle
115	87	59	31	3				Celibacy
116	88	60	32	4				Craftsmanship / Artisan
117	89	61	33	5				Discernment / Distinguish Spirits
118	90	62	34	6				Encouragement
119	91	63	35	7				Evangelism
120	92	64	36	8				Exhortation
121	93	65	37	9				Faith
122	94	66	38	10				Giving
123	95	67	39	11				Healing
124	96	68	40	12				Helps / Service
125	97	69	41	13				Hospitality
126	98	70	42	14				Intercession / Prayer
127	99	71	43	15				Knowledge
128	100	72	44	16				Leadership
129	101	73	45	17				Mercy / Compassion
130	102	74	46	18				Miracles
131	103	75	47	19				Missionary
132	104	76	48	20				Music

133	105	77	49	21				Pastoring / Shepherding
134	106	78	50	22				Poverty (voluntary)
135	107	79	51	23				Prophesy
136	108	80	52	24				Teaching
137	109	81	53	25				Tongues (interpreting)
138	110	82	54	26				Tongues (speaking)
139	111	83	55	27				Wisdom
140	112	84	56	28				Writing

Analysis Instructions

Analysis:

1. First, look over the Analysis Sheet to make sure you have entered a number from 1 to 10 in each of the 140 pre-numbered Response boxes. If you left any of the boxes empty, go back to the corresponding question(s) and enter your Response.

2. Now, unfold the Analysis sheet. Calculate the sum of the 5 Responses in each horizontal row and enter it in the Sum column. You need to do this for each of the 28 rows of Responses. Each sum should be a number between 5 and 50.

3. Next, look over the 28 numbers you have just entered in the vertical Sum column. Look for the highest number you can find (for example 47). Now, place an "A" in the Rank column for the row with the highest Sum. If there is more than one row with this same high number, place an "A" in the Rank column for each.

4. (If you placed an "A" in 3 or more Rank boxes, then skip this step) - Look for the second highest number (for example 43). Place a "B" in the Rank column for each row with this number.

5. (If you placed an "A" or "B" in 3 or more Rank boxes, then skip this step) - Look for the third highest number and place a "C" in the Rank column for each row with this number.

6. Now look at the names of the Spiritual Gifts / Talents beside the Rank boxes where you entered "A", "B", or "C". These are the Spiritual Gifts and Talents that it seems God has given to you.

7. You can find out more about your Spiritual Gifts and Talents by reading the Spiritual Gifts Reference Material on the following pages. If you are reading this document on a computer with Internet access, clicking on any Bible verse reference will open a window containing that Bible verse. After reading the verse, you can close the Bible window to return to this document.

DISCOVERING OUR PERSONALITY STYLE THROUGH TRUE COLORS

Outcomes

In this module participants will :

- Discover the qualities and characteristics of their own particular personality style or type;

- Gain an understanding of other personality styles.

Key Concepts

- True Colors is a metaphor.
- Each person is a unique blend of the four colors or styles—a spectrum.
- There are no bad or good colors.
- There are wide individual variations within each color spectrum.

Each of us has a different and unique personality; however, there are commonalities that we share. True Colors is an attempt to identify various personality styles and label them with colors. This model of categorizing personality styles is based on many years of work by other researchers and psychologists. Essentially it draws heavily on the work of Isabel Briggs-Myers, Katherine Briggs, and David Keirsey. Don Lowry, a student of Keirsey, developed the system called True Colors which uses four primary colors to designate personality types and behavioral styles.

Lowry's objective was the application of temperament or personality style to facilitate deeper communications and understanding. He hoped it would result in positive self- worth and self-esteem. The True Colors program was designed to maximize the application of psychological style in the workplace, in the family and in education and in other types of communities. The ease of understanding and use in all human relationships and interactions make this model very functional.

The belief is that with increased understanding of ourselves and others that conflict will decrease. Once you learn your color and that of your co-workers, you will have a better understanding of why they behave the way they do!

Each color is associated with certain personality traits or behaviors. Everyone has some degree of each color, but one color is predominant. The following quiz will identify your color spectrum. Print out the following two pages. Follow the directions carefully and transfer your scores to the score sheet. If you have two colors with the same score, you pick which one you think more accurately describes you.

Instructions: Compare all 4 boxes in each row. Do not analyze each word; just get a sense of each box. Score each of the four boxes in each row from most to least as it describes you: 4 = most, 3 = a lot, 2 = somewhat, 1 = least.

Row 1	A Active Variety Sports Opportunities Spontaneous Flexible	B Organized Planned Neat Parental Traditional Responsible	C Warm Helpful Friends Authentic Harmonious Compassionate	D Learning Science Quiet Versatile Inventive Competent
	Score [ ]	Score [ ]	Score [ ]	Score [ ]
Row 2	E Curious Ideas Questions Conceptual Knowledge Problem Solver	F Caring People Oriented Feelings Unique Empathetic Communicative	G Orderly On-time Honest Stable Sensible Dependable	H Action Challenges Competitive Impetuous Impactful
	Score [ ]	Score [ ]	Score [ ]	Score [ ]

Row 3	I Helpful Trustworthy Dependable Loyal Conservative Organized	J Kind Understanding Giving Devoted Warm Poetic	K Playful Quick Adventurous Confrontive Open Minded Independent	L Independent Exploring Competent Theoretical Why Questions Ingenious
	Score	Score	Score	Score
Row 4	M Follow Rules Useful Save Money Concerned Procedural Cooperative	N Active Free Winning Daring Impulsive Risk Taker	O Sharing Getting Along Feelings Tender Inspirational Dramatic	P Thinking Solving Problems Perfectionistic Determined Complex Composed
	Score	Score	Score	Score
Row 5	Q Puzzles Seeking Info Making Sense Philosophical Principled Rational	R Social Causes Easy Going Happy Endings Approachable Affectionate Sympathetic	S Exciting Lively Hands On Courageous Skillful On Stage	T Pride Tradition Do Things Right Orderly Conventional Careful
	Score	Score	Score	Score

Total Orange Score	Total Green Score	Total Blue Score	Total Gold Score
A,H,K,N,S	D, E, L, P, Q	C, F, J, O, R	B, G, I, M, T

If any of the scores in the colored boxes are less than 5 or greater than 20 you have made an error. Please go back and read the instructions.

Congratulations! You now know your color spectrum. Here are some general descriptions of each color.

Greens	Oranges
Are innovative and logical	Are free and spontaneous Are
Seek to understand the world	impulsive risk-takers Are active
Need to be competent Require	Are optimistic Resist commitment
intellectual freedom Are	Can become virtuosos Thrive on
curious	crises
Question authority	Are drawn to tools
Push themselves to improve	Like to be the center of attention
Seek perfection in play	Have great endurance
May become intellectually	Are drawn to action jobs Need
isolated Are slow to make	variety
decisions	Are dynamic, animated
Value concise communication	communicators
Look for intellectual stimulation	Are competitive
Enjoy intriguing discussions	Deal with the here and now Are
Are sometimes oblivious to	bold in relationships Are
emotions	generous
Are detached Believe work is	Have difficulty finding
play	acceptance Like to live in a
Are drawn to technical	casual atmosphere Bring
occupations Analyze and	excitement to society
rearrange systems Focus on	
the future	
Bring innovation to society	

Golds	Blues
Are dutiful and stable Need to be useful	Are in search of themselves
	Need to feel unique
Want to be self-sufficient Value organization Desire punctuality	Must be true to themselves Look for symbolism
Schedule their lives	Value close relationships
Make and keep commitments	Encourage expression
Measure worth by completion	Desire quality time with loved
Are goal-oriented	ones Need opportunities to be
Value rules	creative Compromise and
Prepare for the future	cooperate Nurture people, plants
Are inclined to join groups	and animals Look beyond the
Believe work comes before	surface
play Safeguard tradition	Share emotions
Prefer order and cleanliness	Make decisions based on
Are responsible and dedicated	feelings Need harmony
Are drawn to respected	Are adaptable
occupations	Are drawn to literature
Enjoy positions of authority	Are drawn to nurturing careers
Desire structure	Get involved in causes
Bring stability to society	Are committed to ideals Bring unity to society

http://hsgd.org (Head Start of Greater Dallas)

APPENDIX 5

SAMPLE EMPLOYMENT CONTRACT

This agreement is made and takes effect on MM/DD/YYYY between (company), a (State) corporation, hereafter called "Company" and (employee), hereafter called "Employee".

1. The Company hereby employs Employee for a term commencing on the date of this agreement and Employee hereby accepts such employment.

2. During the Employee's employment he/she will:

    A. Devote such time and effort as may be reasonably required by the Company to perform his/her duties.

    B. Not engage in any other employment or business activity without the Company's written consent.

    C. Perform such duties as may reasonably be requires of him/her by the Company.

3. For services rendered by the Employee, the Company shall pay him/her as follows:

    A. The annual sum of $X, calculated as follows (insert compensation formula)

    B (Optional) A bonus of ($X, Y% of sales, etc.) payable (monthly, quarterly, annually) based upon (performance goals)

    C. (Optional) Non-payroll benefits to include health insurance, travel and business entertainment expenses, and other items specified in Attachment A.

4. Employee agrees that during his/her term of employment by the Company and for a period of one year after termination of such employment, he/she will not act as an employee, agent, broker, shareholder, or otherwise engage in any business selling

products similar to those customarily sold by the Company within the States of (specify).

5. Employee understands that he/she will acquire confidential information of business value to the Company during the course of his/her employment. Employee hereby agrees not to divulge such confidential information to any other party, or to use such information for his/her own profit except in performance of employment activities beneficial to the Company.

6. This agreement is an employment-at-will agreement. The Company may, at any time, with or without cause, discharge the Employee by giving him/her written notice of such discharge.

7. Employee's employment shall terminate upon his/her death; inability or failure to perform the duties required by his/her employment; or his/her written notice of resignation given to the Company.

8. Following termination of employment, all obligations under this agreement shall end except for the provisions of items 4 and 5, and any causes of action which may arise from the circumstances of the termination.

9. This agreement constitutes the entire agreement between Company and Employee.

10. This agreement shall be interpreted and, if necessary, adjudicated in accordance with the laws of (State, County).

11. Until written notice of other address(es) are exchanged between the parties, all notices legally required shall be deemed delivered by the sending of registered mail to the following addresses:

Company address

Employee address

In witness to their agreement to these terms, Company's representative and Employee affix their signatures below:

APPENDIX 6

GENERAL PARTNERSHIP AGREEMENT

This agreement ("Agreement") establishes a partnership ("Partnership") between the following parties:

{names and addresses of all people who will be in the partnership}

and is undersigned and set forth this {date} of {month}, {year}.

The undersigned parties hereby agree to the following provisions as conditions of the Partnership:

SECTION 1--Partnership Outline

1.1 The Partnership will be named {name of partnership}, for the purpose of {purpose of the partnership}, and will conduct all business at {address where business will be conducted}.

1.2 Partnership will commence on the date listed above, and will end {specific date Partnership will terminate, and/or a clause about how the Partnership will end, such as mutual agreement on a dissolution, death of one or more partners, etc.} .

SECTION 2--Initial Capital

2.1 Each Partner will contribute original capital according to the following rules: {description of how much each partner will contribute to the initial capital}.

2.2 A separate capital account will be maintained for each Partner.

SECTION 3--Interest on Capital

{detail if/when Partners may collect interest on their initial capital contributions}

SECTION 4--Shares

Each Partner's shares in the Partnership shall be determined by {method of determining shares, such as making them proportional to the amount of initial capital each Partner contributes}.

SECTION 5--Accounts/Income

5.1 Each Partner will have an income account in his/her individual name, which shall be separate from the capital account mentioned in Section 2.

5.2 Income and/or salaries will be distributed {description of if/when any income and/or salaries will be distributed to Partners, including a description of how the income and salaries will be determined}.

SECTION 6--Profits and Losses

6.1 Any profits and/or losses will be distributed and/or debited from a Partner's income account.

6.2 Profits and losses will be distributed and/or debited {description of when profits and losses will be accounted for; monthly, quarterly, etc.}.

SECTION 7--Banking

Income and capital accounts for each Partner will be set up {name(s) of bank or institution where accounts will be maintained}.

SECTION 8--Books/Accounting

8.1 Accounting books and other records pertinent to the Partnership will be kept at {location of books}, and any partner and/or his/her representative may have access to the books during normal business hours.

8.2 The accounts for this Partnership will {description of how they will be maintained, included when they will be balanced and whether they will be kept on a cash basis or other method}.

SECTION 9--Management

9.1 Partnership will be managed {description of how the management of the Partnership will work, including any clauses about the day-to-day operations}.

9.2 Each partner is expected to devote (description of how much is expected of each Partner with regard to time spent on the Partnership}.

9.3 Partnership meetings will {outline if/when Partners will be required to attend meetings}.

SECTION 10--Disputes/Arbitration

Disputes that cannot be settled by the Partners via a mutual decision-making process will be {sent to an arbitrator, voted on, etc.}.

SECTION 11--Partner Withdrawal or Death

11.1 Should a Partner wish to leave the Partnership, {process by which a Partner may leave, including what happens to his/her contribution} .

11.2 Any remaining partner {may/may not} purchase the withdrawing Partner's interest in the Partnership. This process will be governed by the following rules: {description of process for one Partner "buying out" another}.

11.3 Upon a Partner's death {outline of what happens should one Partner die unexpectedly, such as whether his/her heirs receive his/her interest in the Partnership, if one Partner can buy the interest, if the interest will be distributed equally among remaining partners, etc.} .

11.4 Partners may mutually agree to remove one or more members if {conditions under which Partners may remove a member, such as fraud, embezzlement, imprisonment, etc. Also include the process by which this removal should occur.} .

SECTION 12--Confidentiality/Non-Compete

12.1 Any information that involves the Partnership, directly or indirectly, shall be considered Confidential. No Partner may share this Confidential Information with any third party without the written consent of all other Partners.

12.2 Should a Partner leave the Partnership, willingly or unwillingly, he/she shall not take any position, nor engage in any activity, at any company, organization, etc. that is deemed a competitor to the Partnership, for a period of {number of days, months, years, etc.}.

SECTION 13--Jurisdiction

This Agreement is subject to the laws and regulations of the state of {State}, as well as any applicable federal laws.

We, the undersigned, agree to all the provisions listed above, and sign this document of our own free will.

Signed:

_____   _____
Partner Name   Partner Name

_____   _____
Partner Signature   Partner Signature

APPENDIX 7

SAMPLE BOOKING AGREEMENT

This agreement is made on MM/DD/YY between _____ (hereafter "Presenter") and (hereafter "Performer"), represented in this matter by _____ (hereafter "Manager") acting as Performer's agent. Presenter hereby engages Performer to provide the Performance generally described below under the following terms:

All persons engaged to provide the Performance are named in Attachment A.

The Manager's name, address, telephone number(s), and email address are:

The Presenter's name, address, telephone number(s), and email address are:

The date and time of the Performance are: _____

The Performance shall take place at: _____

The Performance shall commence at HH:MM am/pm and end at HH:MM am/pm. An intermission lasting X minutes shall be taken by Performer approximately Y minutes after the Performance commences.

The general description of the Performance is:

_____
_____
_____
_____

Presenter shall pay to Performer or Manager the sum of $X immediately following the end of the Performance. Payment shall be by check payable to _____.

Any tips or other payments made to Performer by third parties shall not be deducted from this fee.

Presenter shall make every effort to prevent any recording or transmission of the Performance without the written permission of Performer or Manager.

Presenter and Performer shall be excused from their obligations hereunder in the event of proven sickness, accident, riot, strike, epidemic, act of God or any other legitimate condition or occurrence beyond their respective control.

Presenter shall be entitled to use the names, likenesses, and other promotional materials provided by Performer or Manager for the purpose of promoting the Performance and attracting attendees.

Presenter shall provide adequate parking space within X feet of the entrance nearest the stage entrance and shall reserve such parking space for Performer's exclusive use from four hours before the starting time of the Performance until three hours after the Performance's ending time.

_____   _____
Presenter's signature   Date

_____   _____
Performer's or Manager's Signature   Date

_____
Presenter's printed name

_____
Performers or Manager's printed name

APPENDIX 8

SAMPLE HAIR SALON BOOTH RENTAL AGREEMENT

Name of Salon	
Owner's Name	
Salon Address	
Phone Number	
Stylist's Name	
Address	
Phone Number	

Rental Provisions

- Stylist, listed above, is renting a booth/station from Owner, also listed above.

- The rental period will begin on {date} and end {when it will end}.

- Stylist will pay a fee of {amount} every {week, month} for this rental space.

- Payment must be made {by a certain date, by check, etc.}.

- Stylist will be an independent contractor, not an employee of the salon.

- Stylist will conduct his/her business during the normal business hours of the salon.

- Owner will provide {list of what owner will provide for Stylist}.

- Stylist will be responsible for {anything stylist will be responsible for during the rental period}.

- Stylist will, at all times, dress professionally and in a manner befitting the atmosphere of the salon.

- Stylist will maintain a clean and orderly workspace, free of material that may be considered offensive or inappropriate for the environment. Suitability of the material is subject to Owner's discretion.

- Stylist {is/is not} permitted to sublet the rental space.

- Stylist is responsible for any damage to the rental space caused by his/her customers, guests, or by himself/herself.

- This agreement is enforceable under the laws and regulations of the state of {State}.

_____   _____
Stylist Name   Stylist Signature

Date: _____

_____   _____
Owner Name   Owner Signature

Date: _____

APPENDIX 9

SAMPLE BUYER SELLER AGREEMENT

{Detailed description of transaction from Seller to Buyer, including item's year, make, model, and any guarantees}.

The Seller guarantees that the item listed above is free from defects in both materials and workmanship. The item will be under full warranty for {amount of time}. During that time, the Buyer may return the item for a refund, refurbishment, or replacement. Defects, malfunctions, and expenses that do not fall under this warranty are as follows: {list of exceptions}.

The item will be under a limited warranty for {amount of time}. During that time, the Buyer may return the item for repair for the following issues: {list of issues}. Other expenses, damages, and malfunctions will not be considered.

No replacement, refund, store credit, refurbishment, or repair will be considered after the limited warranty period has expired.

_____ _____
(Seller's Signature)   (Buyer's Signature)

_____   _____
(Date)   (Date)

SAMPLE CONTRACT FOR PHOTOGRPAHY SERVICES

Client's Name: _____

Client's Address: _____

Event Location: _____

Event Date: _____ Start Time: _____ End Time: _____

Proof photographs are to be delivered to Client by _____
MM/DD/YYYY

Minimum number of Photographs to be taken: _____

Maximum number: _____

Photographer's Fee: $_____ Deposit paid: $_____

1. The Client shall reimburse Photographer for any additional costs the Photographer may incur for travel, meals, parking, and other reasonable costs necessary to the performance of these services.

2. The deposit is not refundable if the Client cancels or changes the engagement. If the Photographer fails to appear at the place and time specified above, the deposit shall be refunded to the Client.

3. Proof photographs shall be delivered to the Client on CD. The client shall provide the Photographer with a written list of the proof images from which final photographs are to be prepared, and specify the number and format(s) of the final photograph to be delivered for each proof image. See attached Price Schedule for available final photograph formats and their prices.

4. The Client shall assist and cooperate with the Photographer in obtaining the desired photographs, including but not limited to

specifying persons and/or scenes to be photographed; taking time to pose for photographs at the Photographer's direction; providing a person to guide the Photographer to desired persons and/or scenes; pre-shoot consultations, etc. The Photographer shall not be responsible for photographs not taken as a result of the Client's failure to provide reasonable assistance or cooperation.

5. The Photographer retains copyright in the photographs, and hereby grants the Client unlimited but non-exclusive rights to use or reproduce the photographs for which the Client pays.

Applicable Law

The laws of the County of _____ in the State of _____ and any applicable Federal law shall govern this contract.

Signatures

_____   _____
Photographer Signature   Client's Signature

_____   _____
Printed Name

_____
Address

_____
Phone

_____
Address

_____
Phone

APPENDIX 11

SAMPLE WEDDING PLANNER CONTRACT

_____ (hereafter "Wedding Planner"),
_____ (hereafter "Bride") and
_____ (hereafter "Groom", together
hereafter as "Couple") hereby agree to the following terms
concerning the planning of the wedding taking place on

_____
MM/DD/YYYY:

The Wedding Planner will provide # sessions of consultation on
the following dates: _____
_____

The Wedding Planner will provide free rent of the following
wedding items: _____
_____

The Wedding Planner will provide unlimited correspondence via
email and phone for any questions or concerns the Couple has
concerning the coordinating and planning processes.

The Wedding Planner will help the Couple find the following
contacts and will consult with each of them amount of time
before the wedding to verify the contracts and to ensure that all
expense exchanges have been made:

Reverend: {Name}, {Number}, {Officiant Fee}, {Payment Due
Date}

Catering Company: {Name}, {Number}, {Fee}, {Payment Due
Date}

DJ/Band: {Name}, {Number}, {Fee}, {Payment Due Date}

Decorator: {Name}, {Number}, {Fee}, {Payment Due Date}

Florist: {Name}, {Number}, {Fee}, {Payment Due Date}

Ceremony Musician(s): {Name}, {Number}, {Fee}, {Payment Due Date}

Hair/Makeup Stylist: {Name}, {Number}, {Fee}, {Payment Due Date}

Clothing Rental: {Name}, {Number}, {Fee}, {Payment Due Date}

Photographer: {Name}, {Number}, {Fee}, {Payment Due Date}

The Wedding Planner will coordinate the rehearsal dinner, provide an itinerary for all wedding party members and arrange for transportation.

On the day of the wedding, the Wedding Planner will provide the following items and services:

- Unlimited help and consultation   - An emergency bridal kit

- Ensuring that the wedding party is photo-ready -Managing and directing wedding party members and guests throughout the ceremony/reception

- Coordinating with vendors and musicians throughout the night
- Managing any emergencies that arise

The Wedding Planner will receive a total of $_____, with an additional $_____ per guest over the estimated number. This total includes a nonrefundable deposit of _____% ($_____) paid no later than _____MM/DD/YYYY, _____% ($_____) paid by _____ MM/DD/YYYY and the final _____% ($_____) paid no later than _____MM/DD/YYYY. In witness to their agreement to the terms of this contract, the parties affix their signatures below:

_____   _____ _____   _____
Couple's Signatures   Date   Couple Signature   Date

_____   _____
Wedding Planner Signature   Date

APPENDIX 12

SAMPLE SPEAKER'S CONTRACT

This contract is made and entered into on MM/DD/YYYY by the parties named below as Client and Speaker.

Speaker's Information:

Speaker's Name or Business Name:

Address (City, State, ZIP Code):

Phone number:

Fax number:

Email:

Client's Information:

Client's Name or Business Name:

Address (City, State, ZIP Code):

Phone number:

Fax number:

Email:

Speaker's Topic:

Name and address of event venue:

Contact person at event; name, title, phone, email:

Anticipated number of attendees:

Date of Event: _____ Start time: _____

End time: _____

Schedule of intermissions, if any:

Equipment & Room Set-Up Specifications:

[Describe, with graphical aids if necessary, the layout of seats, podium/stage, easel(s), whiteboard, projector, etc., and the specific equipment that Client is to provide at the Client's expense.]

Handouts: a PDF file containing printer-ready handout pages will be emailed to the Client 2 weeks prior to the event date. The Client is responsible for printing and distributing handouts to Client's attendees.

Speaker's Fee

Client shall pay to Speaker a deposit of $_____ no later than 90 days before the event date. If the event is cancelled by the Client, part of the deposit may be refunded according to the following Refund Schedule:

Less than 30 days notice: 0 (zero) per cent of deposit

31 to 60 days notice: 50 per cent

61 or more days notice: 75 per cent

Client shall pay to Speaker $_____, the balance of the Speaker's fee, immediately following the conclusion of the Speaker's presentation.

Expenses

The Client shall arrange and pre-pay for business-class, round trip airline tickets from the Speaker's airport [specify airport] to the venue's airport [specify airport] for the Speaker and 1 (one) Speaker's assistant; ground transportation for the Speaker and assistant between the venue's airport and the Speaker's hotel; dual-occupancy hotel accommodations for the Speaker and assistant from noon on the day before the event until noon on the day the event ends; meals for Speaker and assistant for which receipts are provided; and all other reasonable, documented expenses necessary to the Speaker's conduct of the presentation during the time period of the event.

The Speaker shall submit receipts and an itemized invoice for expenses to the Client within 7 (seven) days of the event's end date. The Client shall reimburse the Speaker with 30 (thirty) days of receiving receipts and invoice.

In witness to their understanding and agreement to these terms and conditions, the parties hereby affix their signatures below.

_____   _____
Client Signature   Date   Speaker Signature   Date

_____   _____
Printed Name   Printed Name

APPENDIX 13

SAMPLE PERFORMANCE CONTRACT

{Name}, henceforth known as "Client," agrees to hire {Name}, henceforth known as "Artist," for a performance at {location} on {date}.

Furthermore, the two parties agree to the following:

Artist will perform {music, magic show, etc.} at {location} on {date}, for a period of {one hour, three hours, etc.}, beginning at {time}.

The performance will specifically consist of {details of the performance}.

Client will pay artist {amount in dollars} as compensation for this performance, payable via {check, money order, cash, etc.} and according to the following plan: {details of the payment, such as any deposit, or any installment plan}.

Setup for the performance will be the responsibility of {Artist or Client}. {If Client is responsible, indicate what he/she will provide, such as sound equipment, for the Artist for this performance}.

Client will provide {additional assistance such as engineers, setup assistants, etc., if applicable}.

Client will also provide {indicate if Artist will be provided with accommodations, if applicable}.

If Client cancels the performance with less than {amount of time} to go until performance date, he/she will pay Artist {amount in dollars}.

Artist may cancel the performance {any conditions under which the artist can cancel, and what will occur if there is a cancellation}.

This contract is enforceable according to the laws and regulations of the state of {State}.

Signed this {date} day of {month}, {year}.

_____   _____
Artist Name   Artist Signature

_____   _____
Client Name   Client Signature

57441774R00205

Made in the USA
Charleston, SC
13 June 2016